Baby Eagle's First Summer

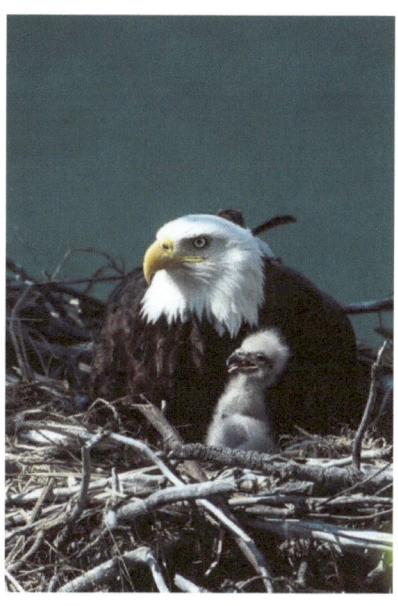

Mark Newman

ISBN-10: 1503209555

ISBN-13: 9781503209558

To Madison, Adeline, Lili and Esko,
who someday will grow up and fledge just like
the baby eagle.

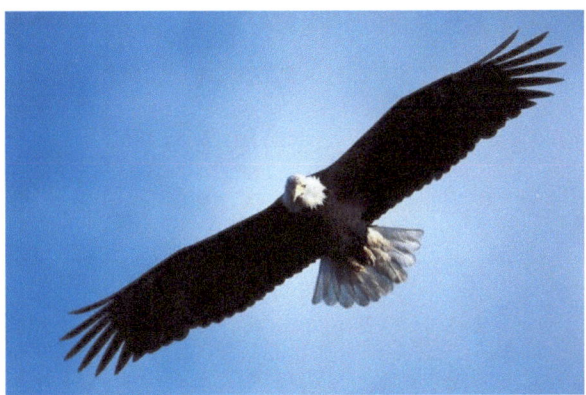

Other Books by Mark Newman

The Majestic Big Cats

Horses of the American West

Bears of the World

My Funniest Friends

Polar Bears

Images from 35 Years of Wandering

Places Near and Far

Animals of the Alaska Zoo

Galapagos: In Darwin's Footsteps

Golden (A Novel)

Kangaroos: The Marvelous Mob

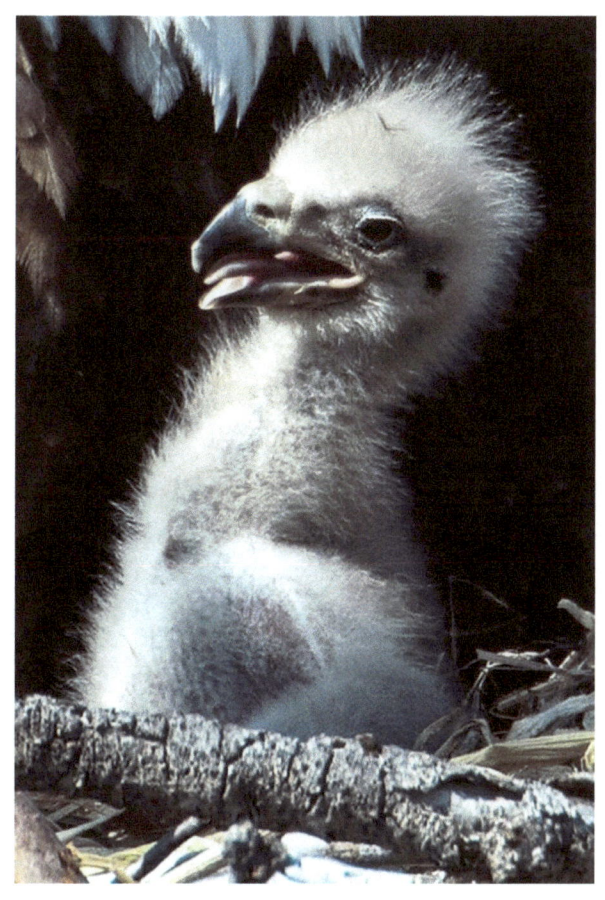

I Hatched Out Just Five Days Ago!

But first I had to spend a full month inside an egg!!

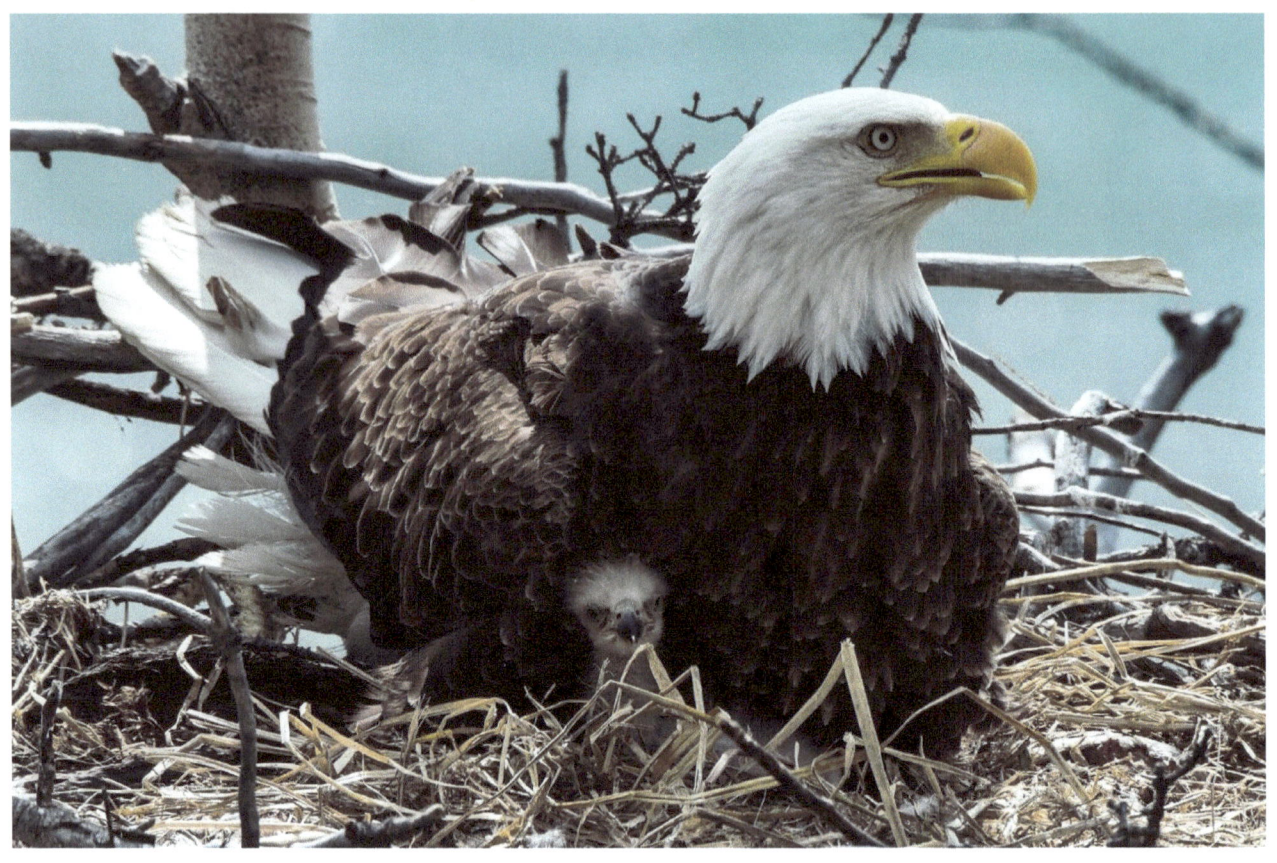

There was a second egg in the nest, but it never hatched. So my mom only has me to take care of.

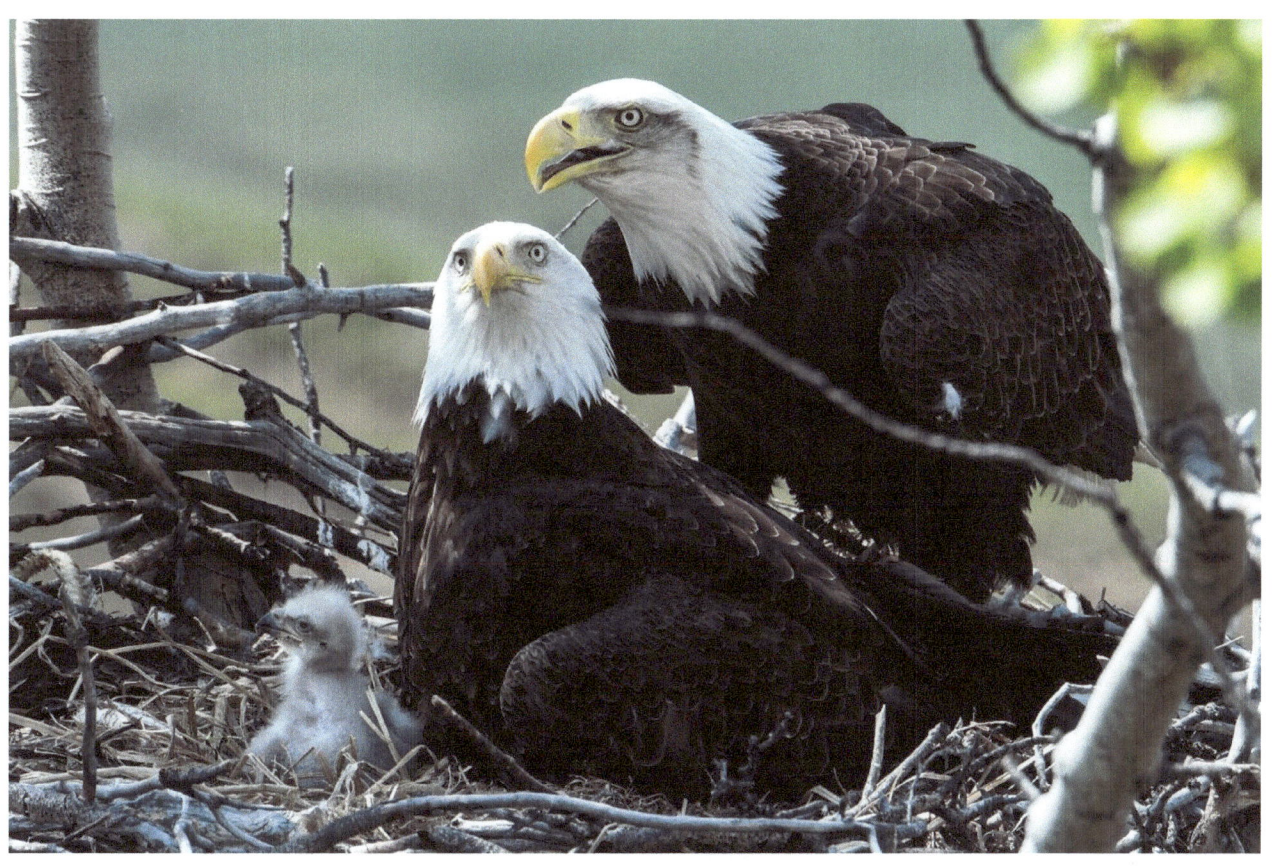

My parents take turns watching me. Sometimes they both stay with me in the nest, but most of the time it's one or the other, either mom or dad.

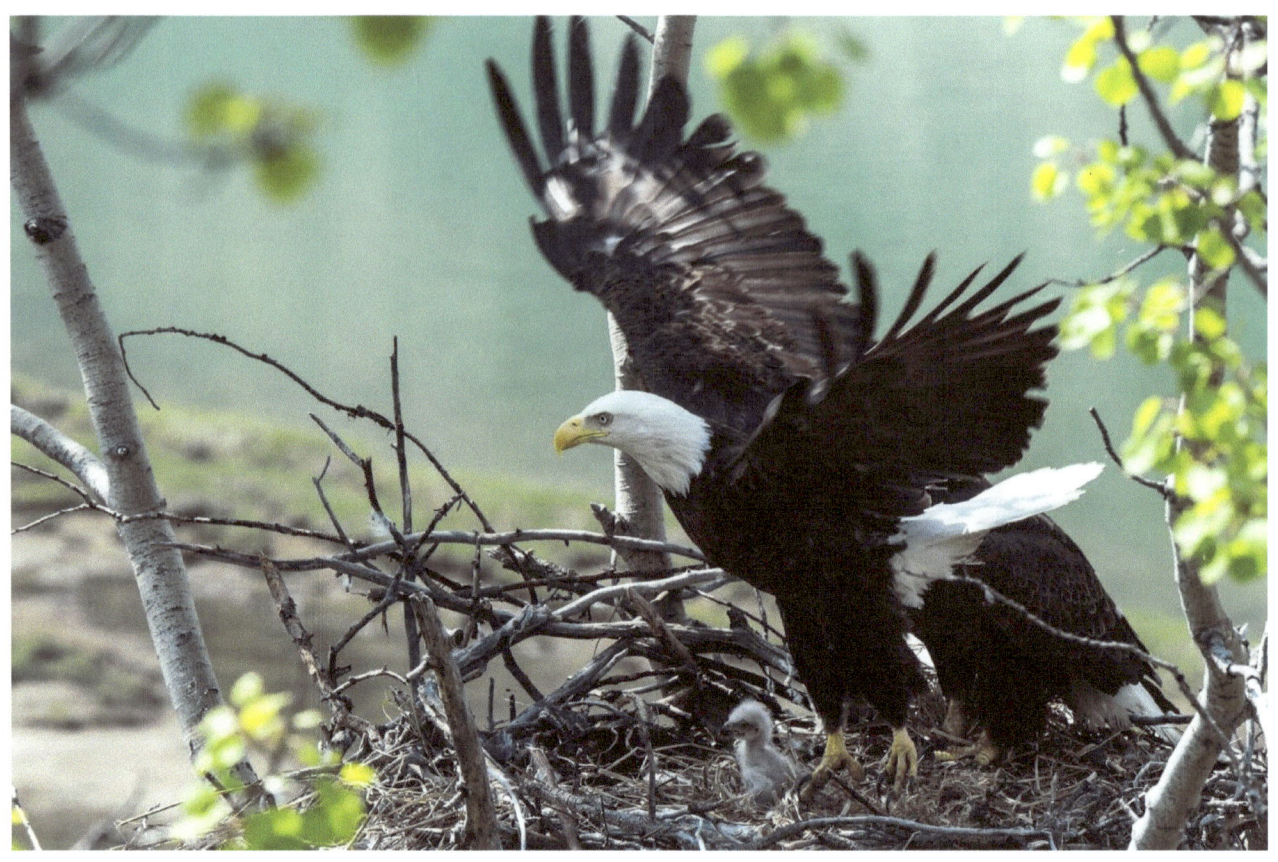

One of my parents stays with me while the other flies off to go fishing. Here my dad is taking off and mom and I will wait for him to bring back a fish.

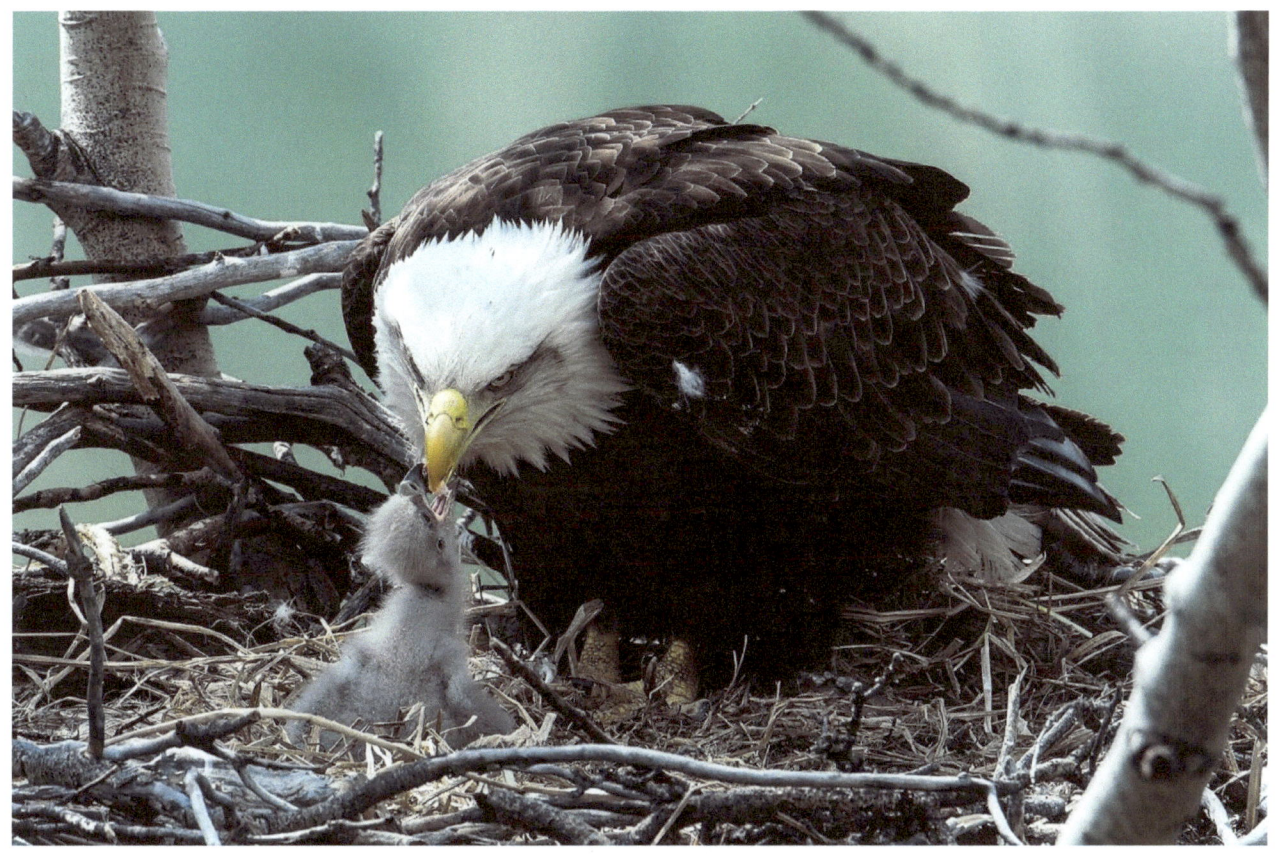

I'm hungry all the time. Dad brought back a fish and mom bit it into tiny pieces and carefully fed it to me.

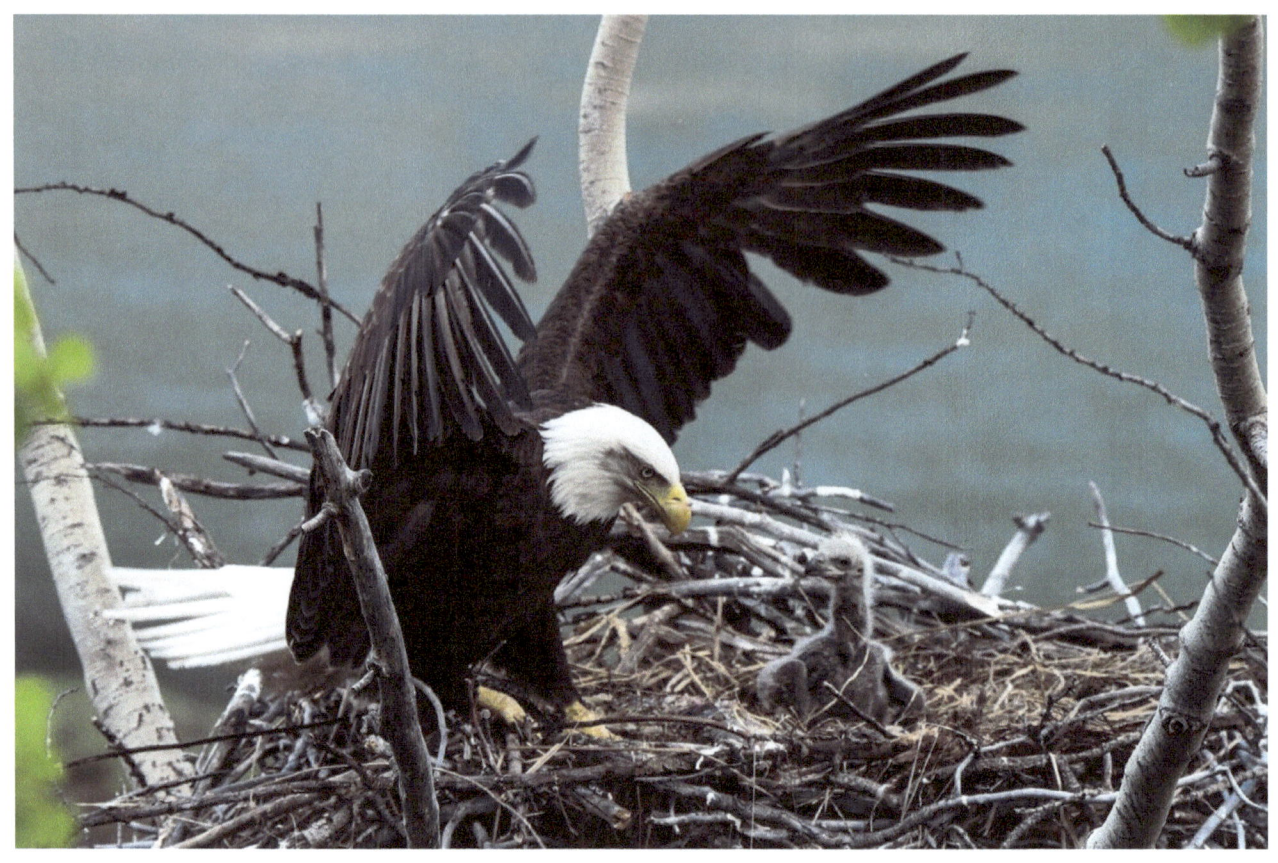

Mom took off to do some more fishing and dad is babysitting me now. He likes to spread his wings to show me how big he is. I am also growing bigger fast.

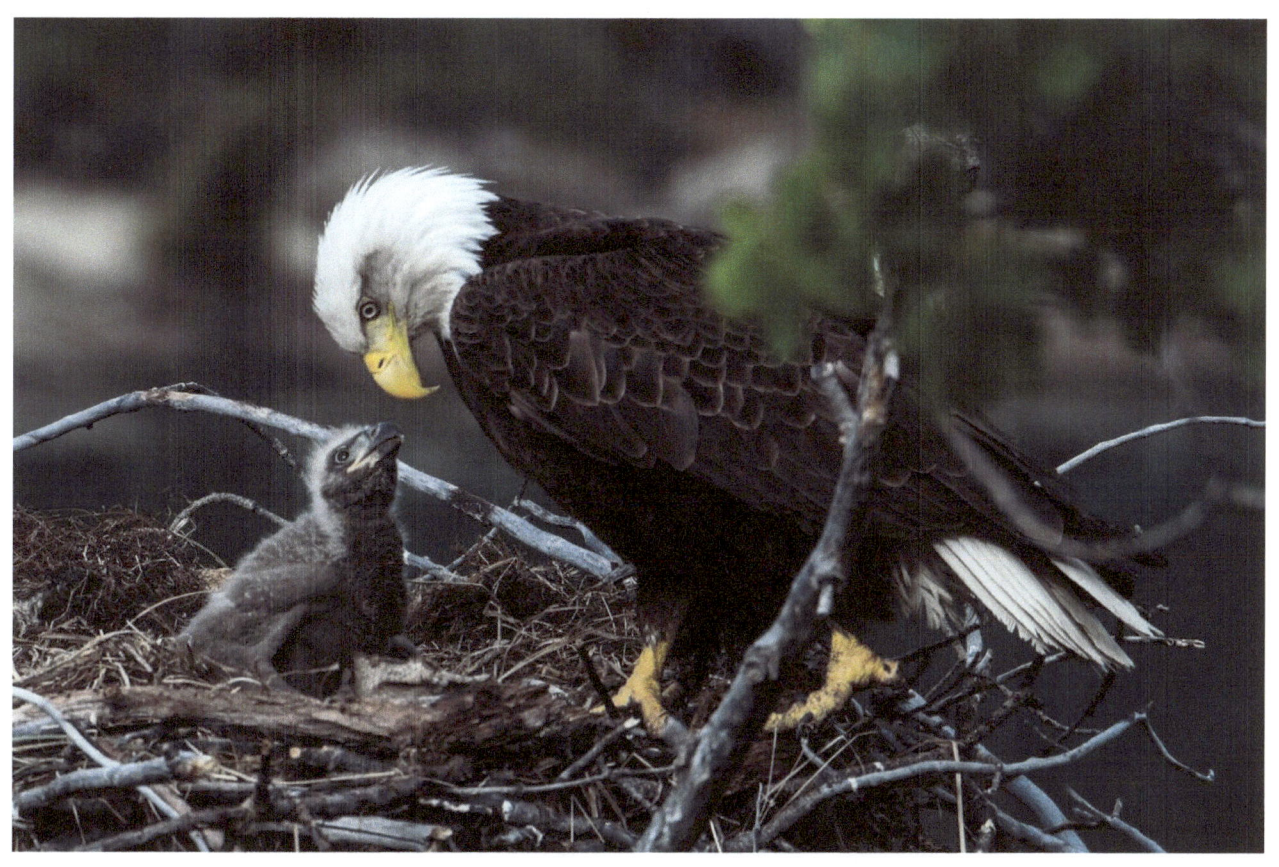

As I grow bigger each day I can see that my feathers are getting darker in color. My parents watch me very closely all the time.

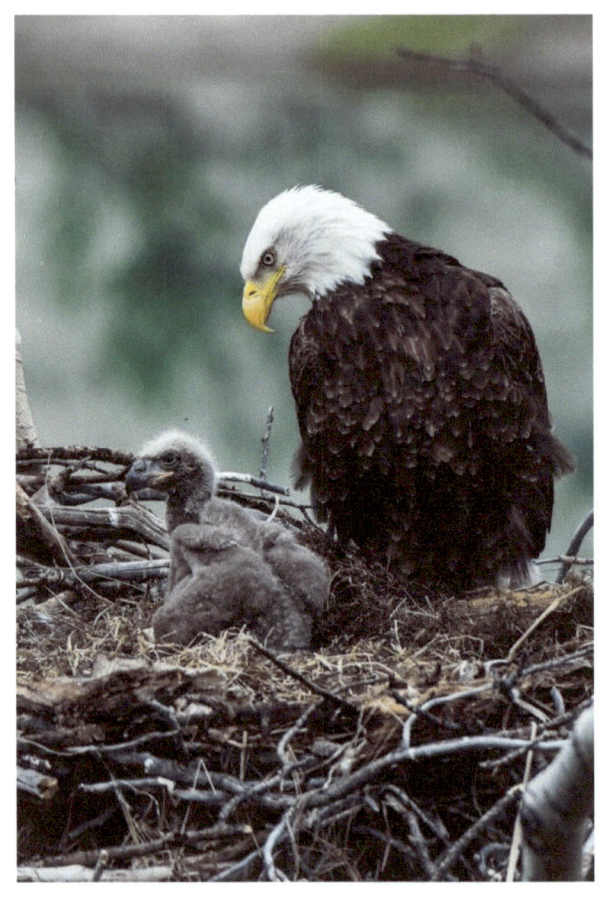

They make sure that I stay healthy and safe. They don't want me to fall because it is a long way to the ground and if I fell there would be no way for me to get back into the nest.

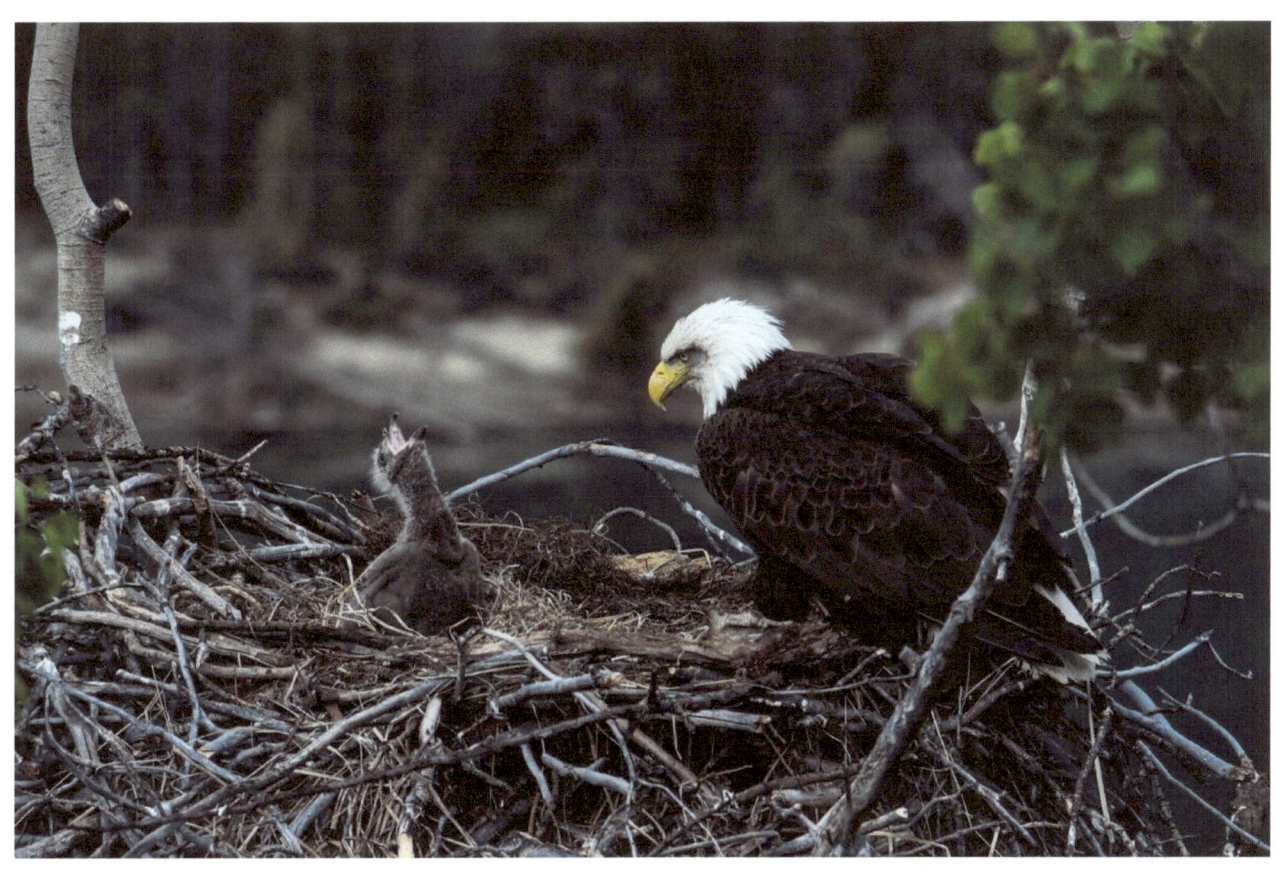

When I'm very hungry I make squeaking sounds to let my parents know.

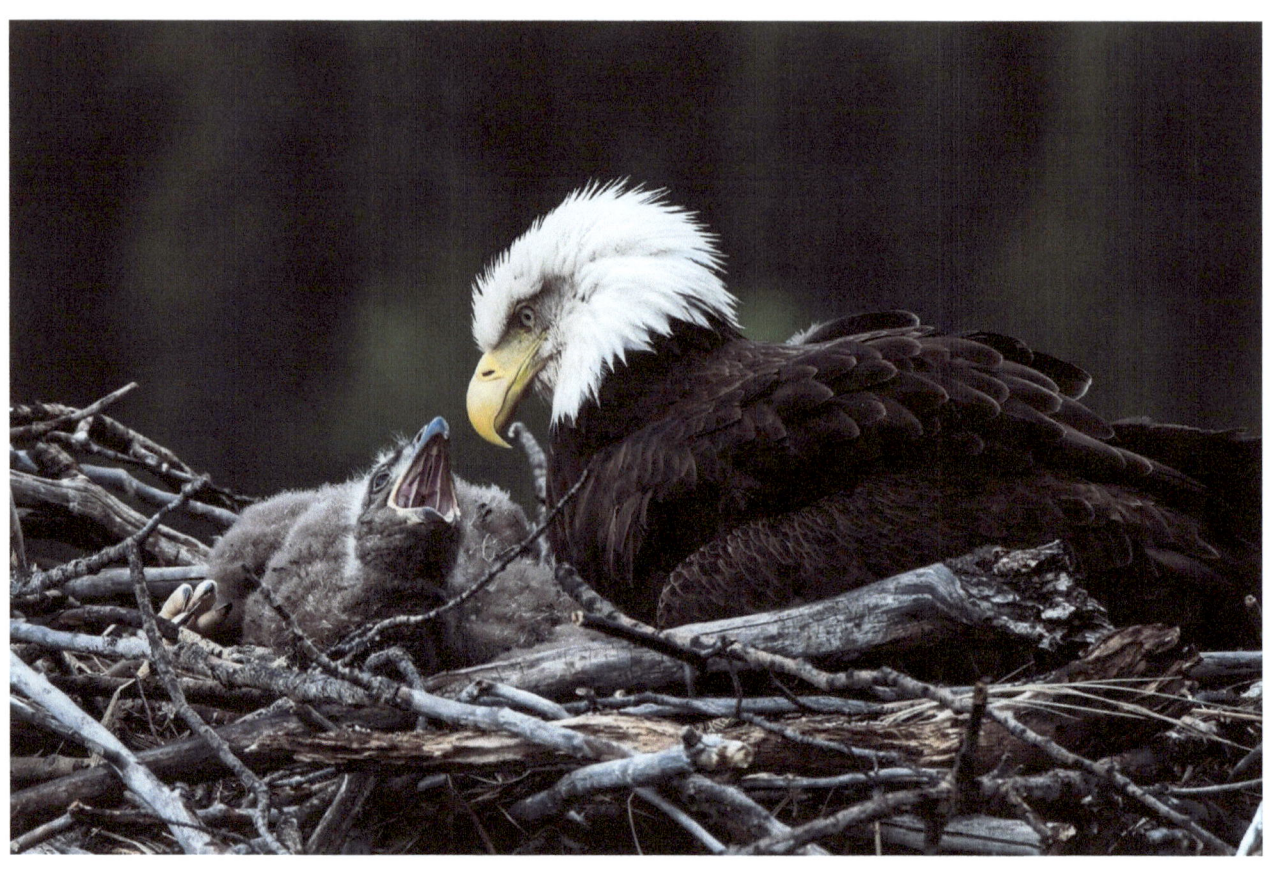

Sometimes they take a long time to catch a fish in the nearby river, so I yell louder and louder. If I could talk like a person I would be saying, "Feed me! Feed me!"

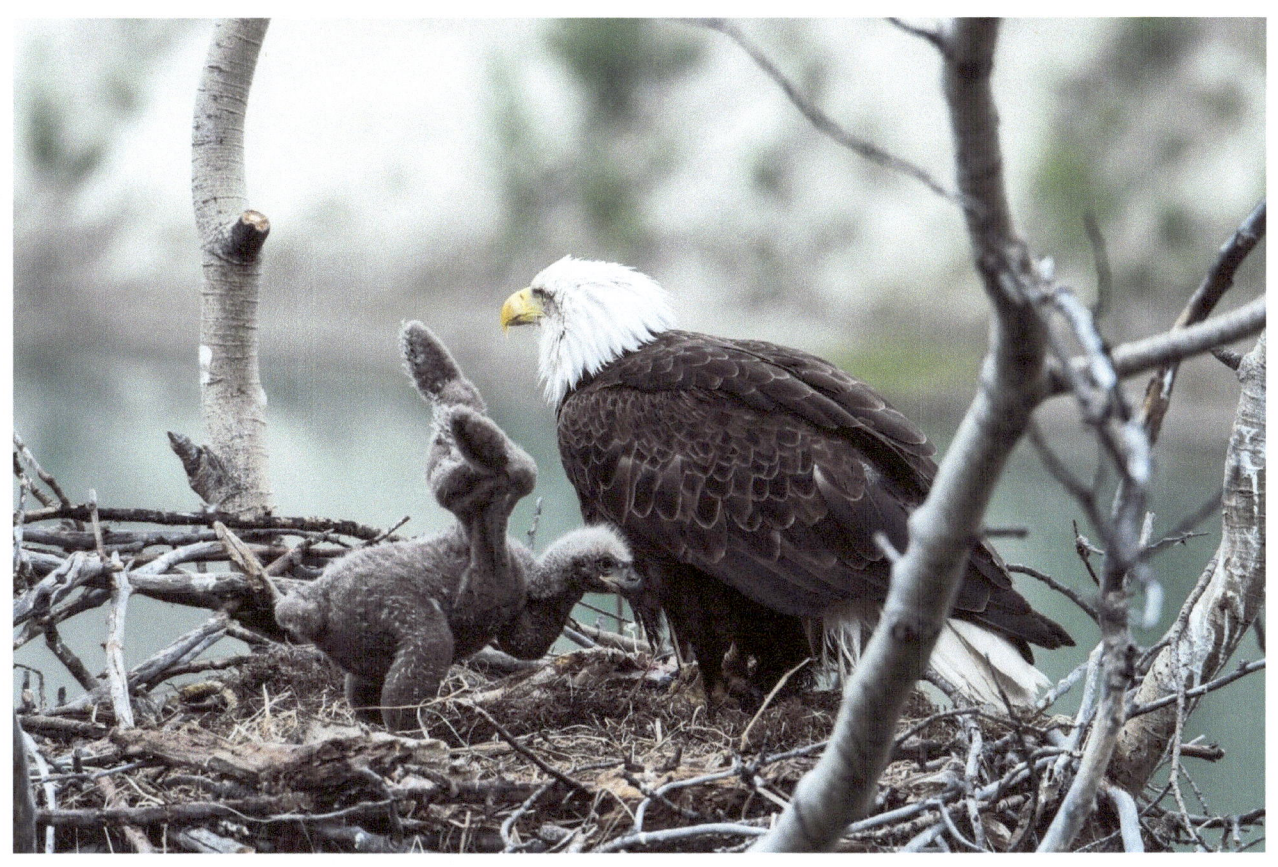

When I turned four weeks old I liked trying out my little wings. I am growing so fast but I don't have any big feathers yet.

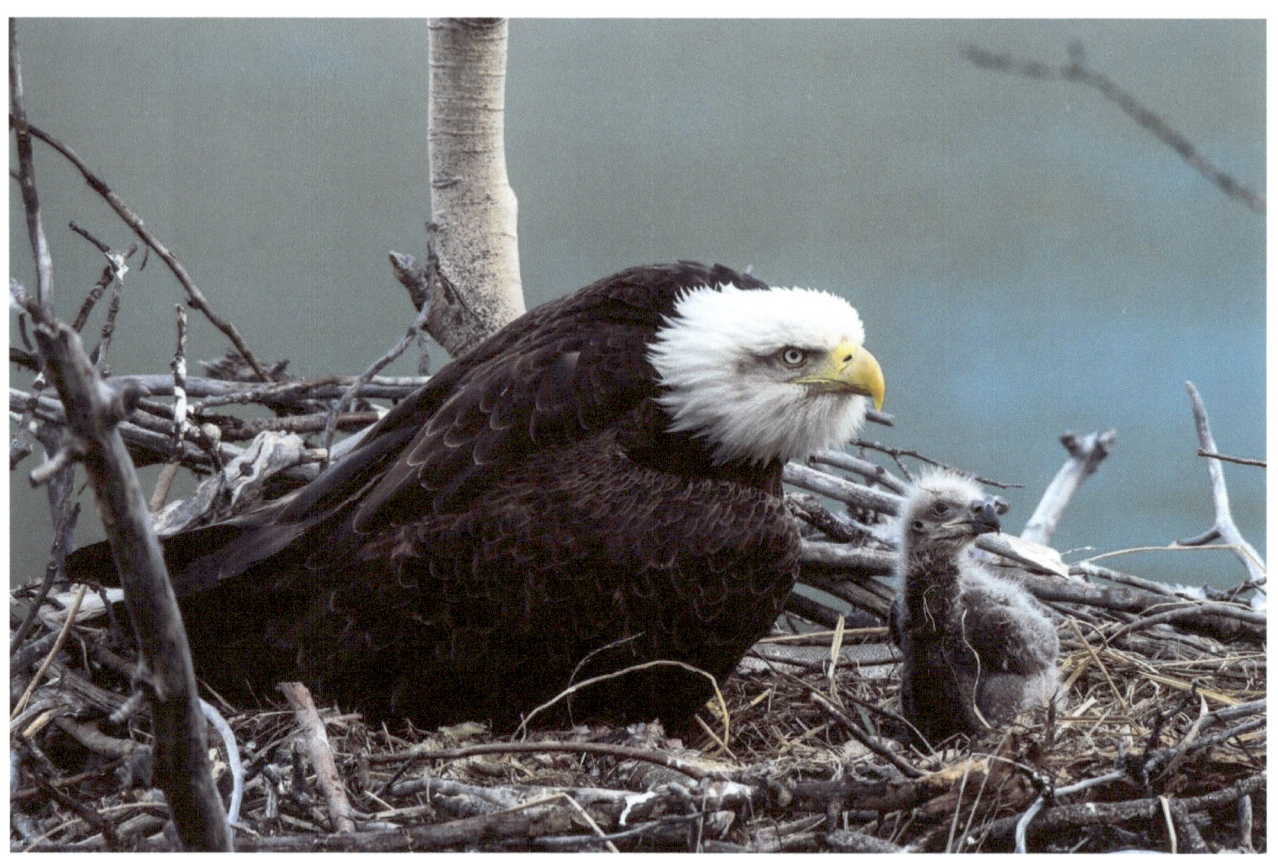

Mom watches out to make sure that no other eagles or hawks fly near to the nest. If she wasn't so careful, then another bird might swoop down and carry me away in its sharp talons.

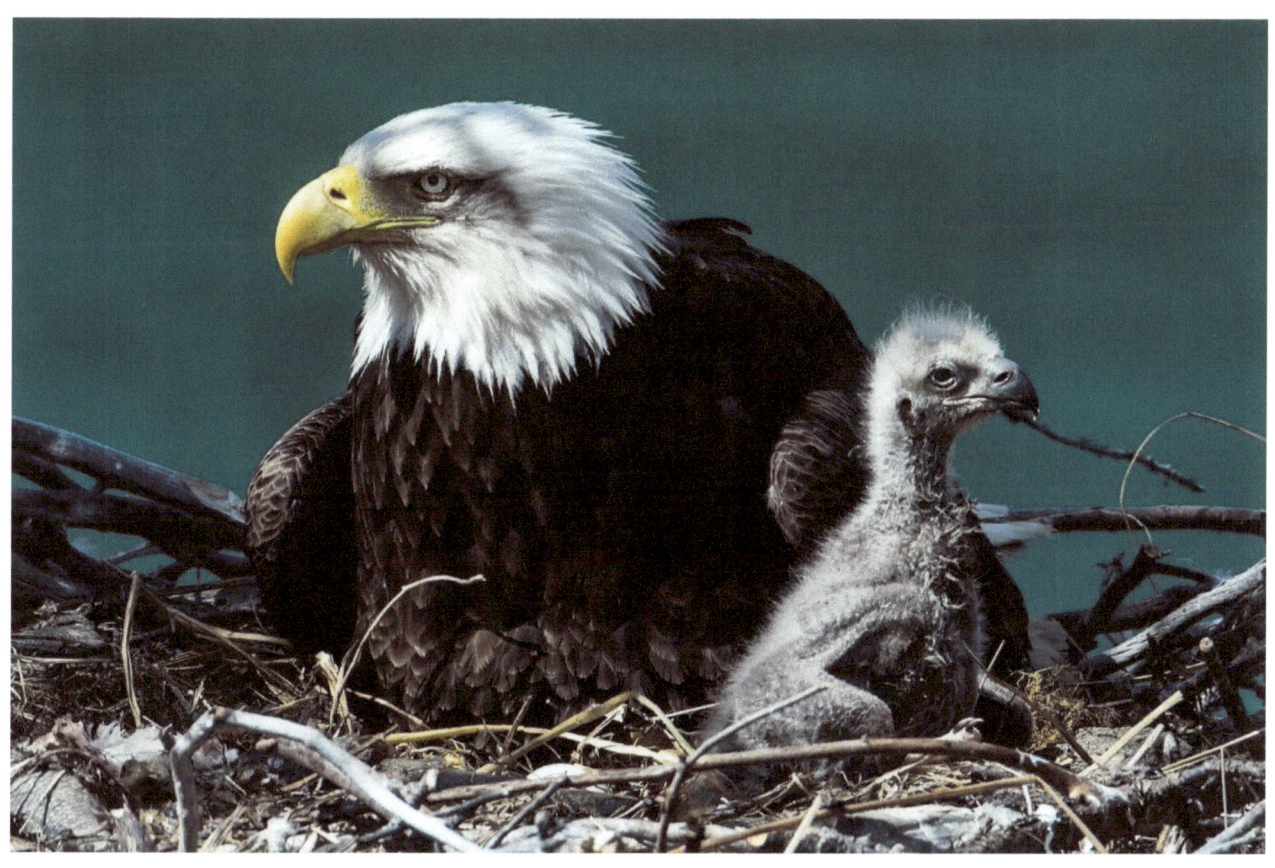

I know that right now I look like a plucked chicken, but in just two more months I will grow to be big and beautiful like my parents.

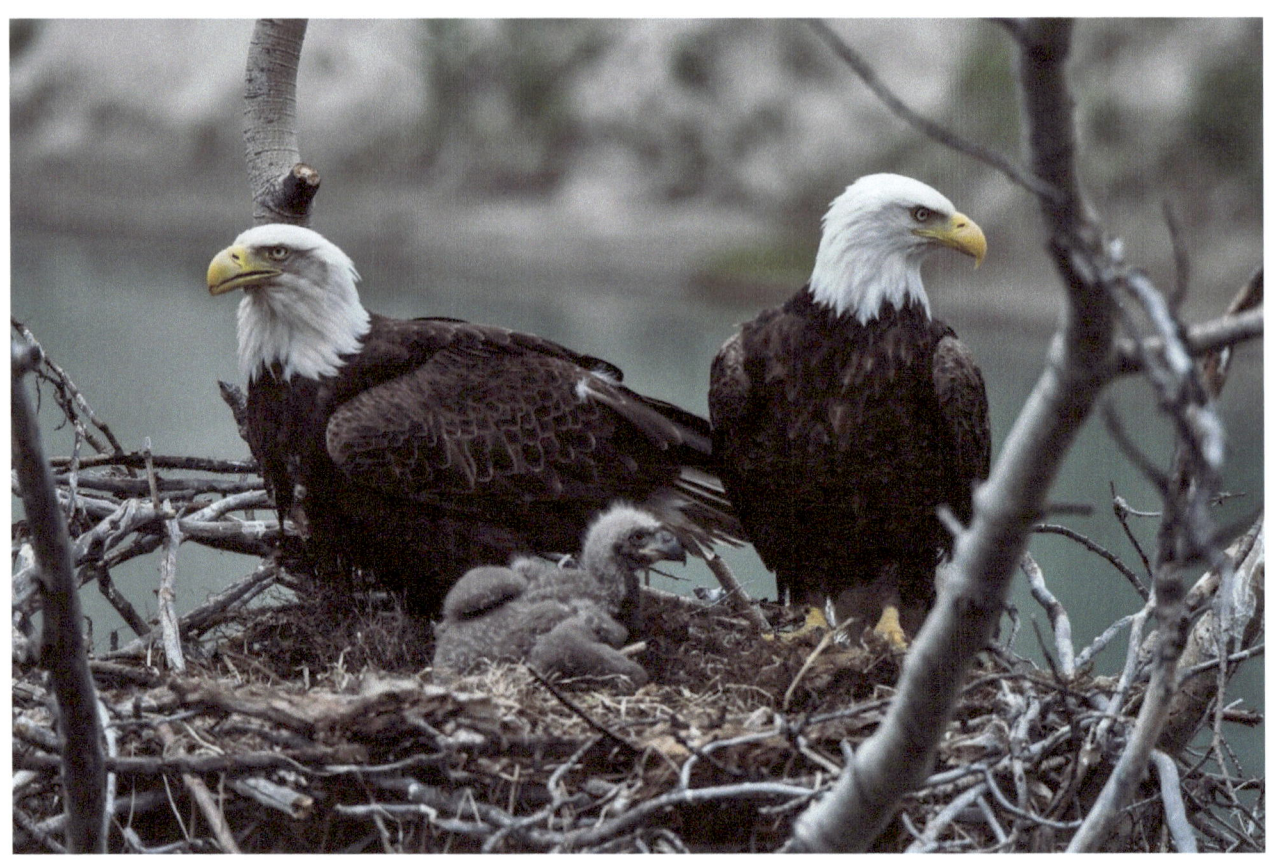

I feel very safe when both of my parents are with me in the nest. They make sure that other eagles stay at least a mile away.

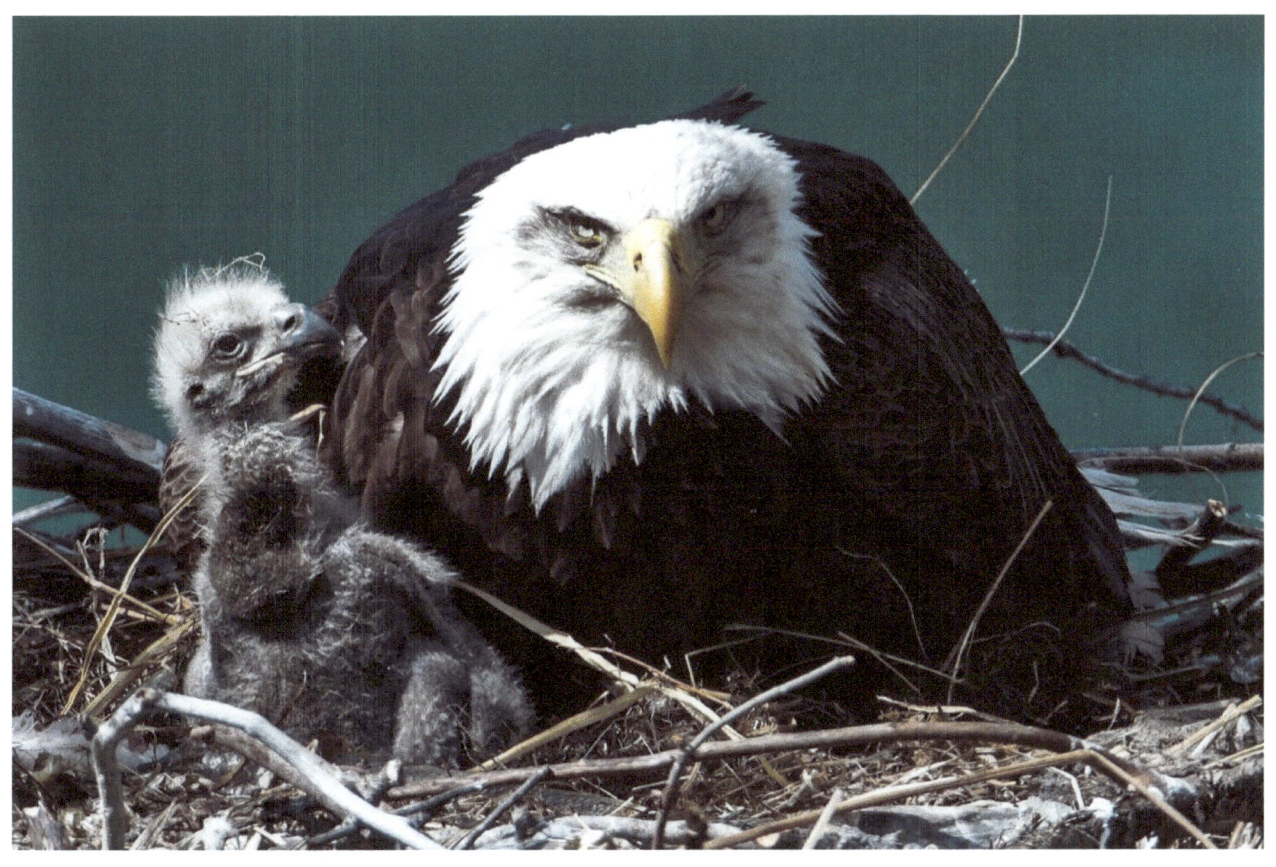

I know that nobody would dare bother me when my mom is around. She is a little bigger than my dad and when she gives you a look, you know not to mess with her.

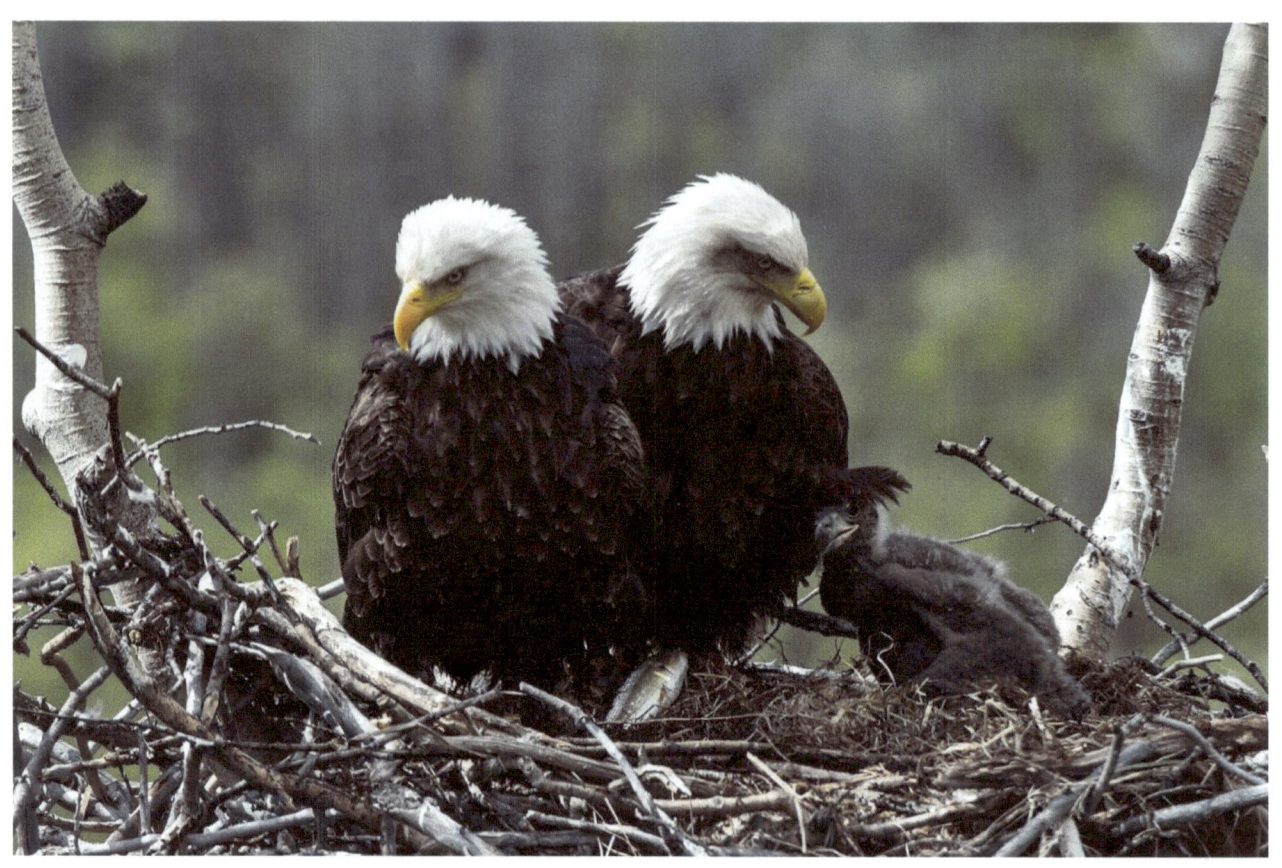

I sometimes tuck under my dad's feathers, either to get out of the rain or for shade on sunny days. His feathers help keep me warm.

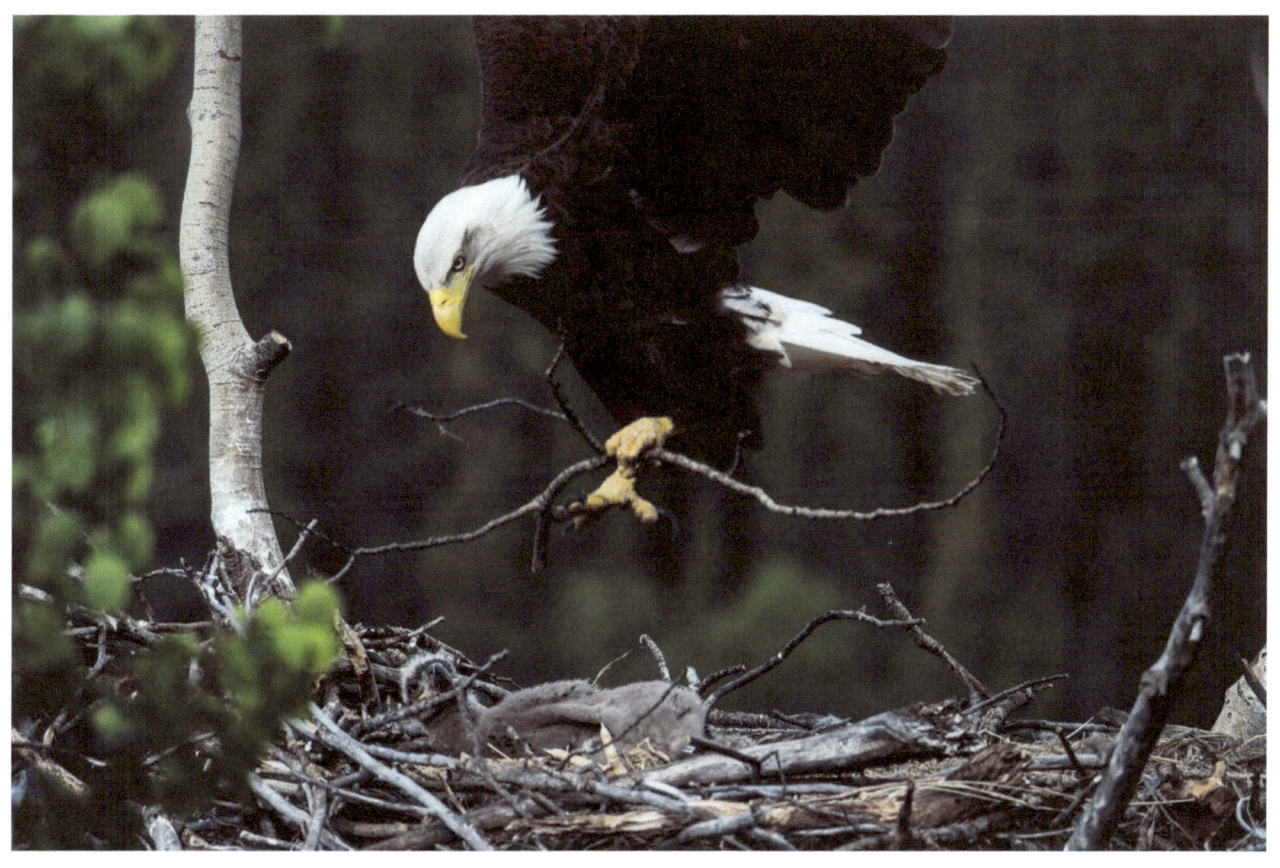

Mom sometimes brings back new twigs to make the nest look better. My parents have been using this same nest for over ten years. There are now so many twigs and branches that the nest weighs over one ton!

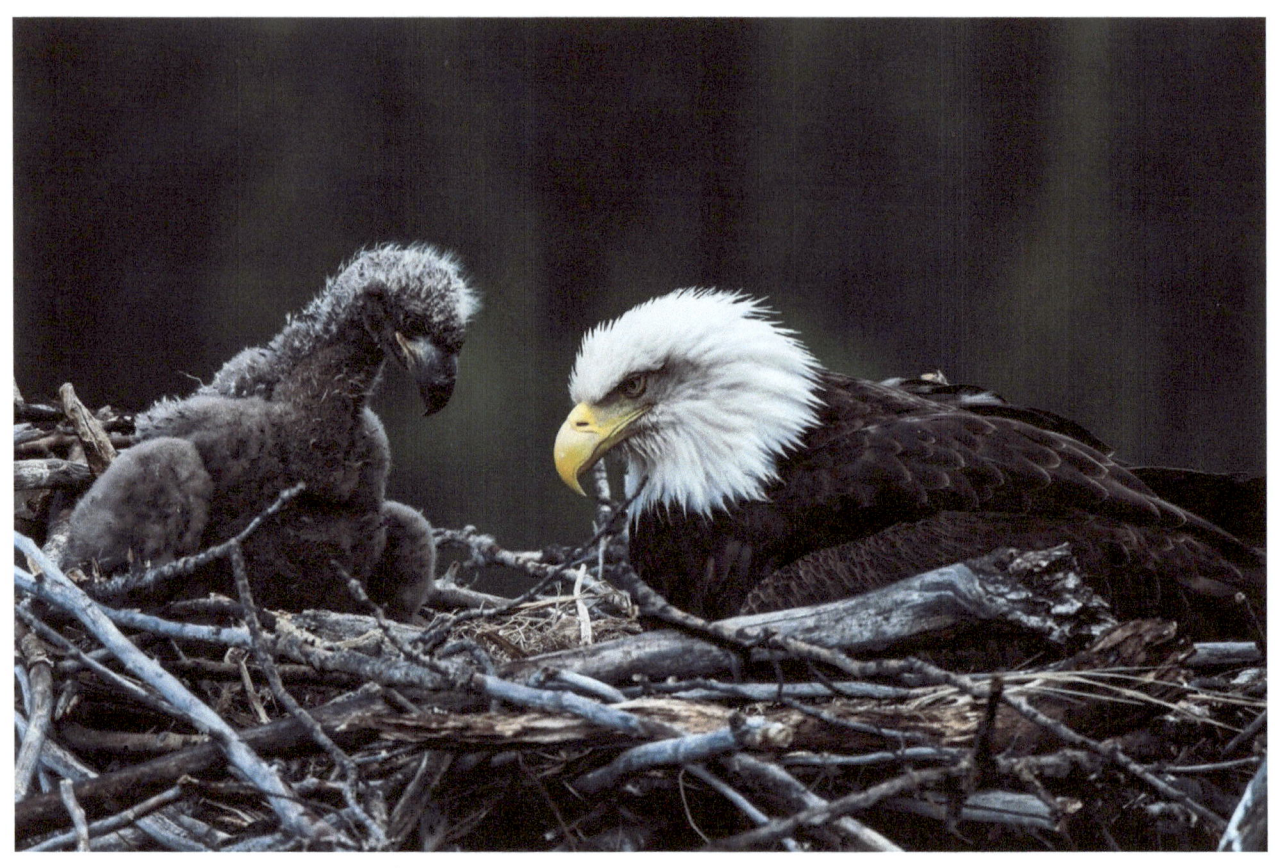

I am now getting big like dad. I feel very healthy and strong because my parents are doing such a good job of feeding and taking care of me.

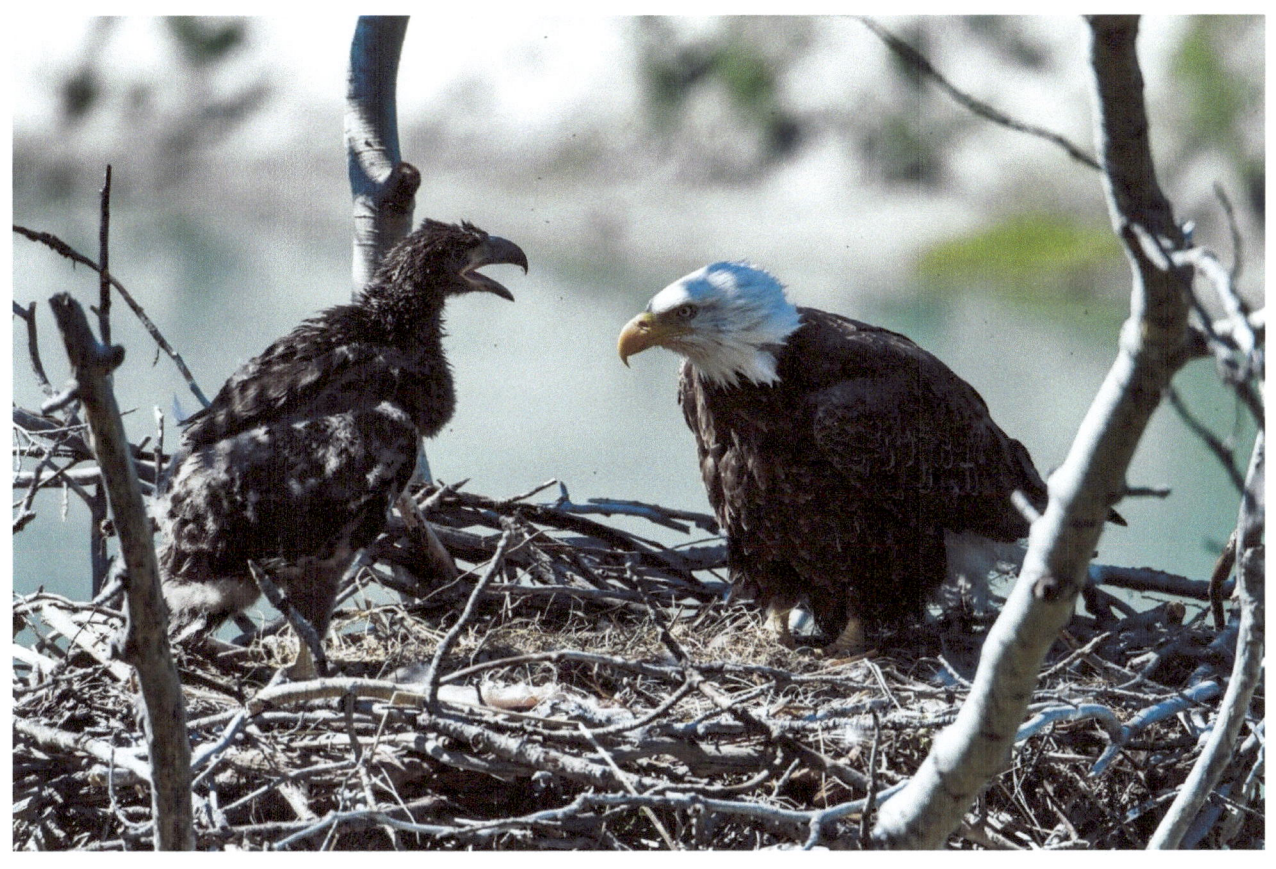

I just keep growing bigger and bigger. I am almost as tall as my parents now that I am two months old. I need lots of food all the time so I can keep growing. Here I am yelling at mom once again to feed me!

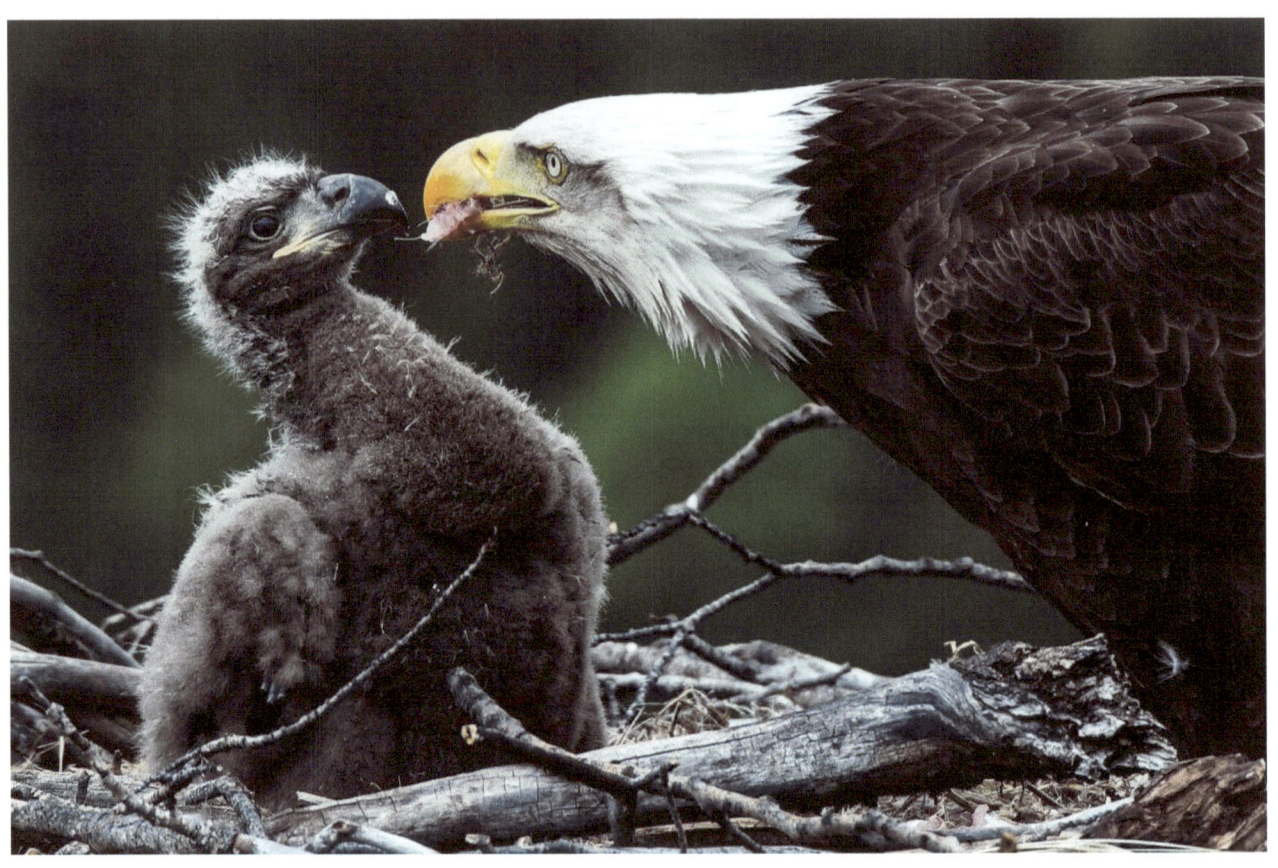

Dad brought back another fish and mom tore it up and has been feeding it to me. I ate so much that I now feel stuffed, but mom keeps trying to force me to eat more.

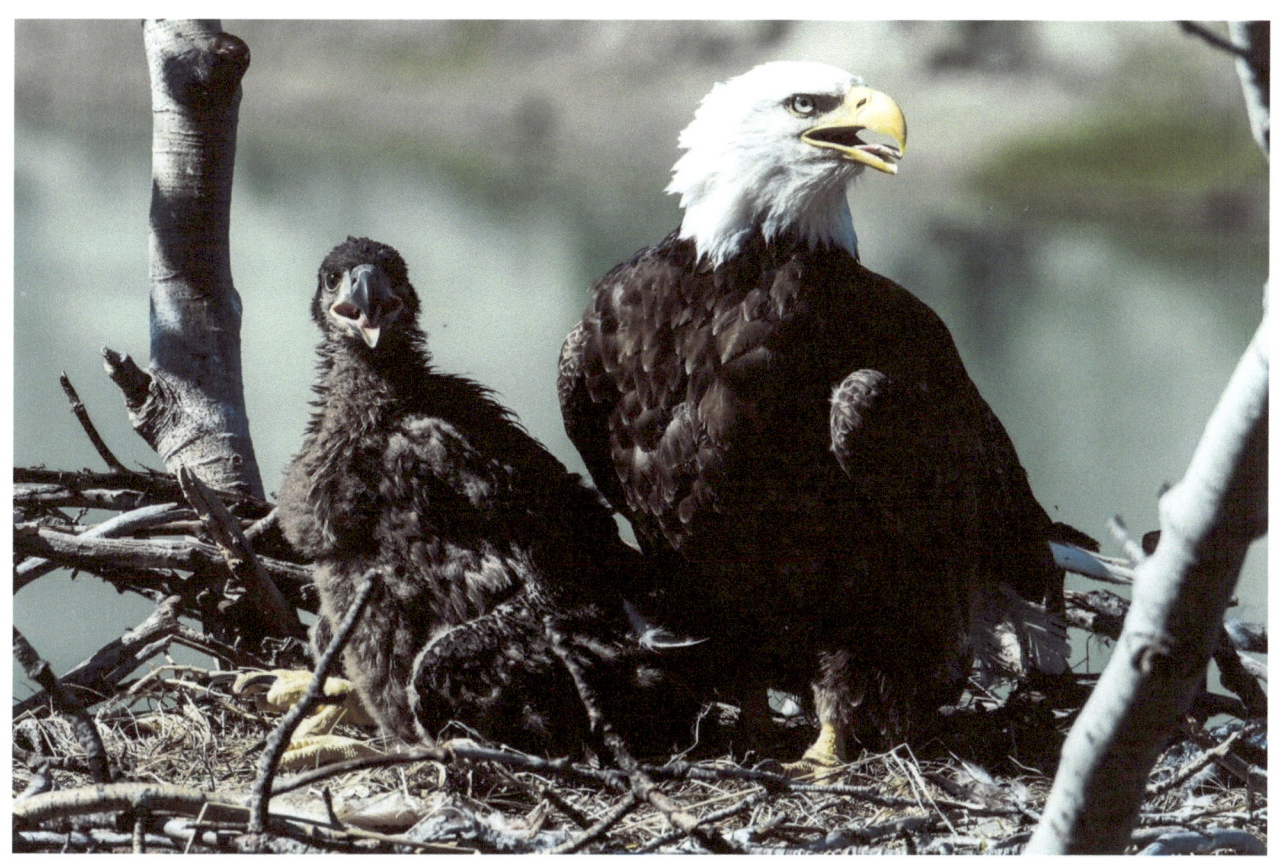

On hot sunny days both mom and I sit around with our beaks open, panting to keep cool. Even though we live way up in the north, the summers can still get plenty warm.

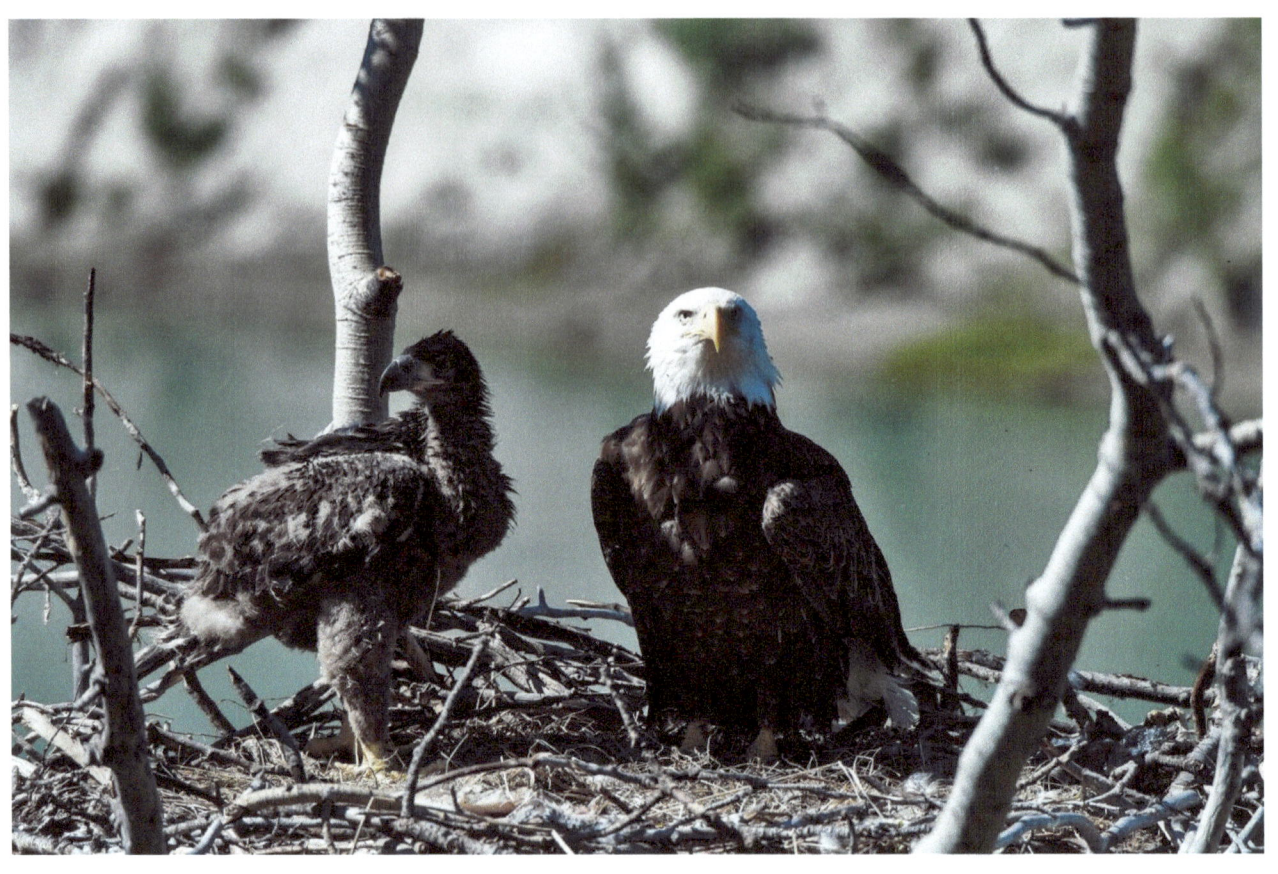

My legs are getting very long. I am getting to feel almost grown up. I even have some big feathers coming in. I can't wait for the day when I can fly like mom and dad.

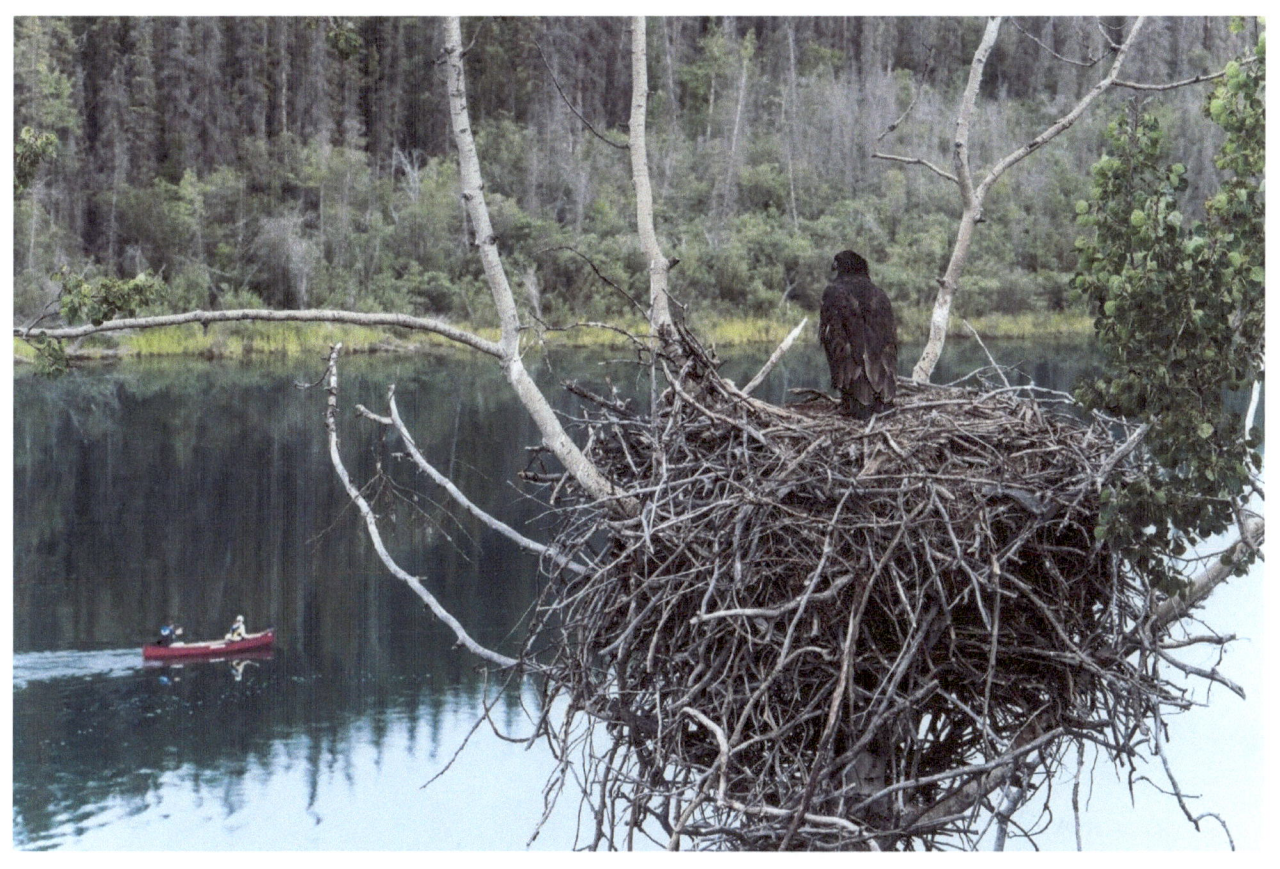

I am old enough now that my parents sometimes leave me alone in the nest. One day while I was looking out over the river a red canoe with two paddlers floated by. They never looked up and didn't know I was watching them.

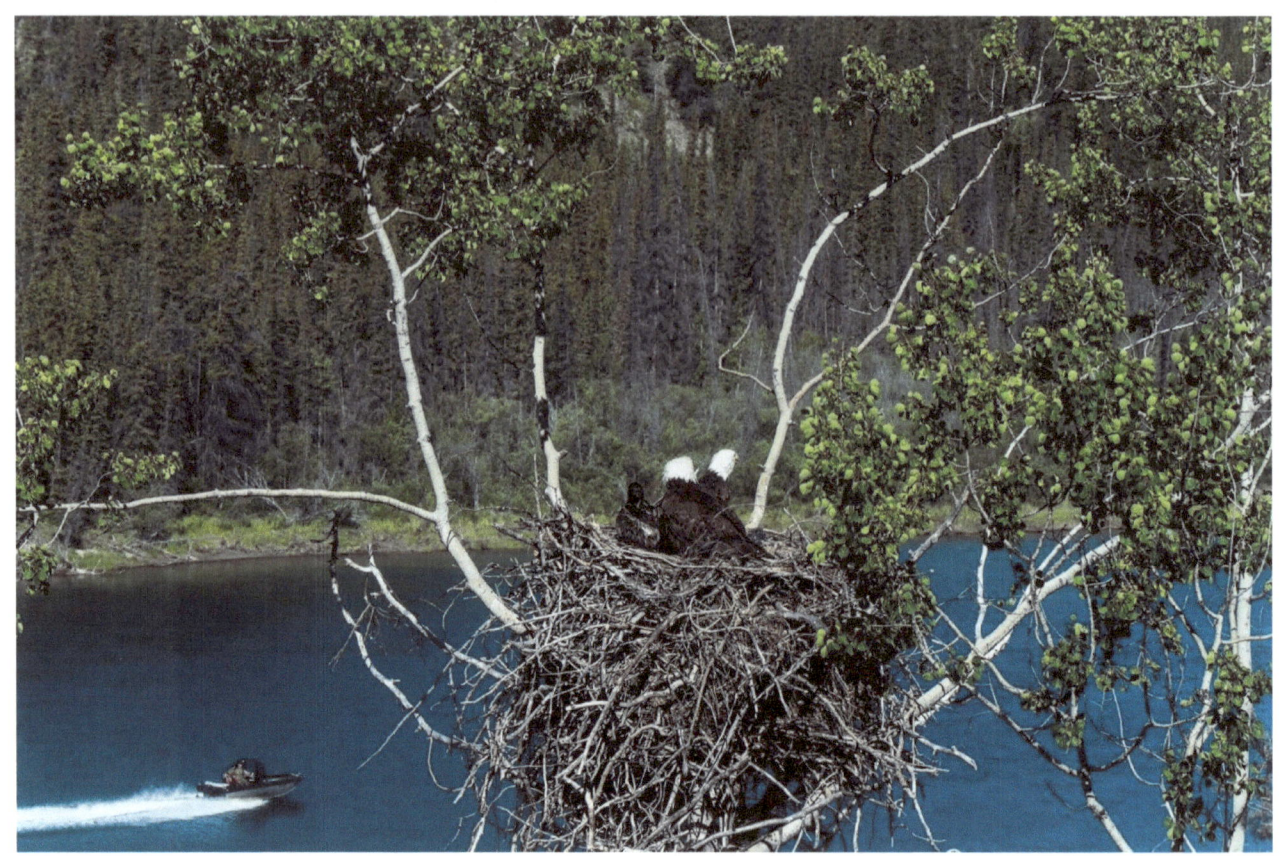

Another time, when both my parents were with me in the nest, a fast motorboat came by, heading down the river. Like the paddlers in the canoe, they never knew we were up here.

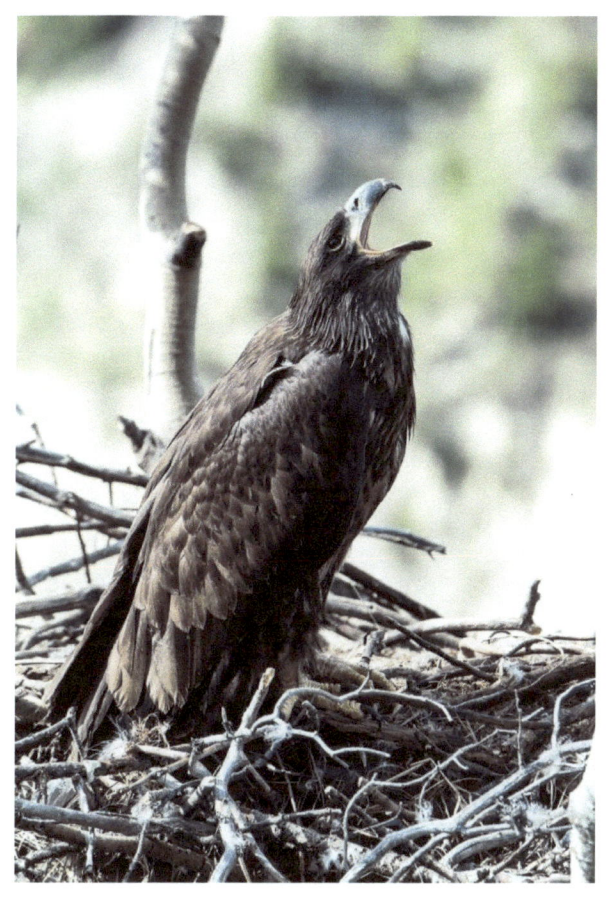

When I am in the nest alone I have to squawk really loudly if I want to call my parents. When I am hungry I do a lot of squawking. Today I hope they will bring back a fish soon. I am so hungry right now!

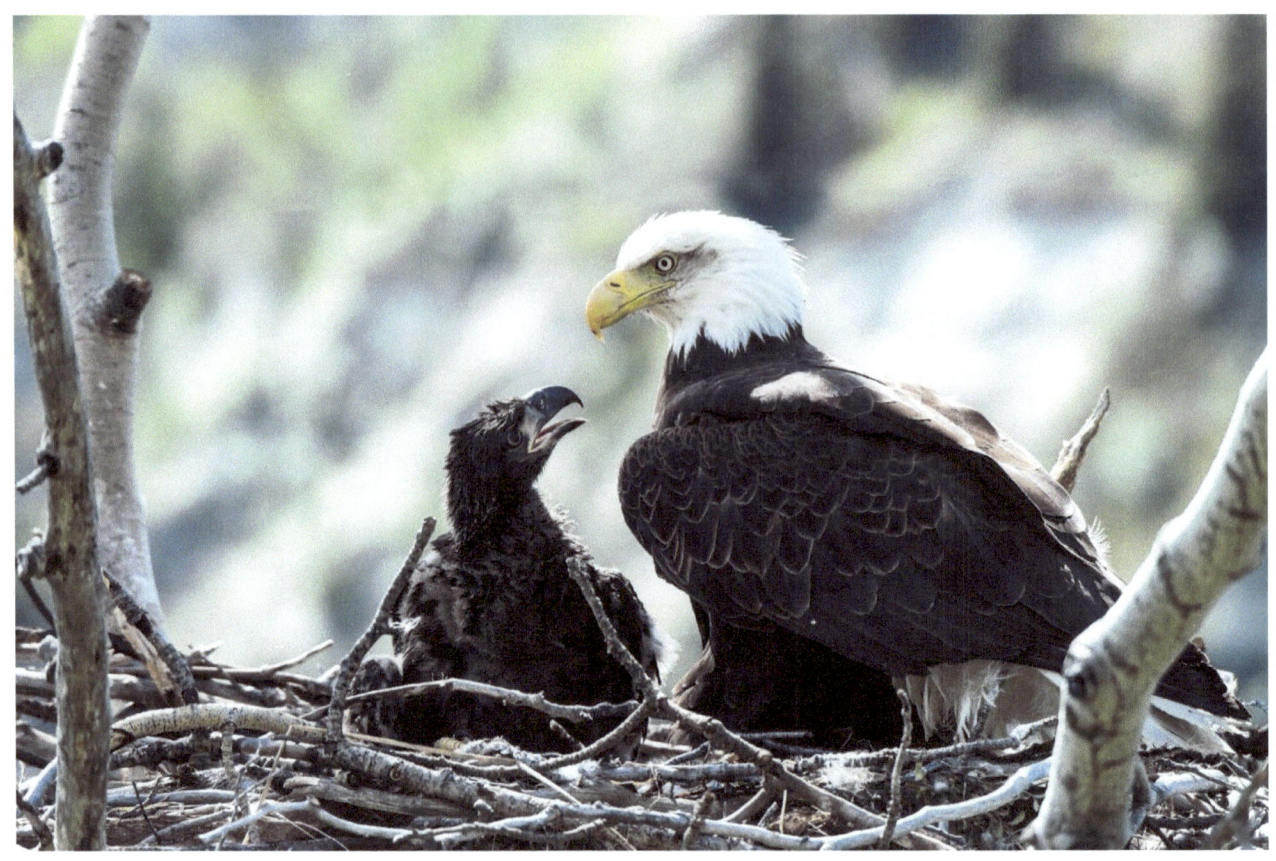

Sometimes my mom or dad will hear me calling and return to the nest without a fish. They want to make sure I am OK but they can't always feed me right away. Fishing is not always easy so I have to be patient.

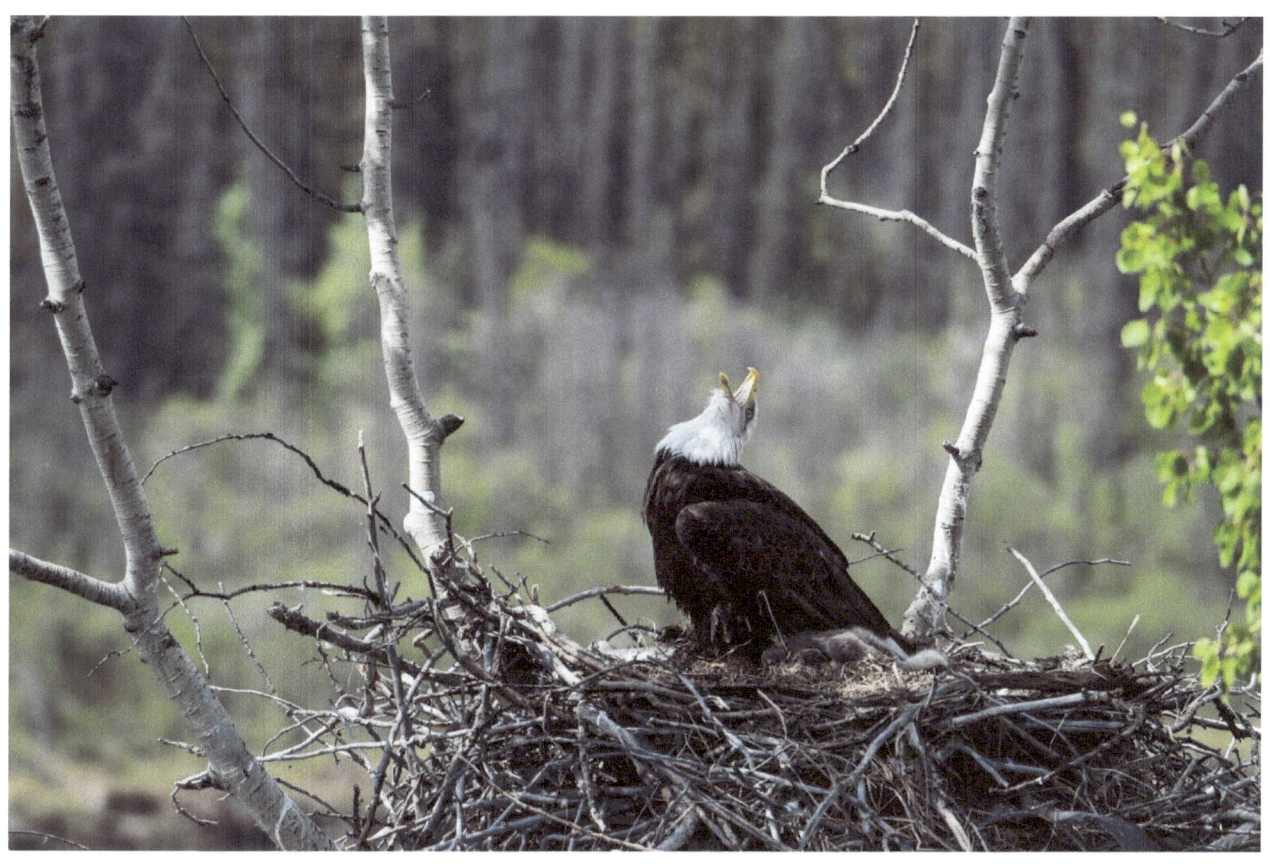

My parents will do a lot of calling when they feel they have been babysitting for too long and they want their partner to be fair and come back and take their turn watching me.

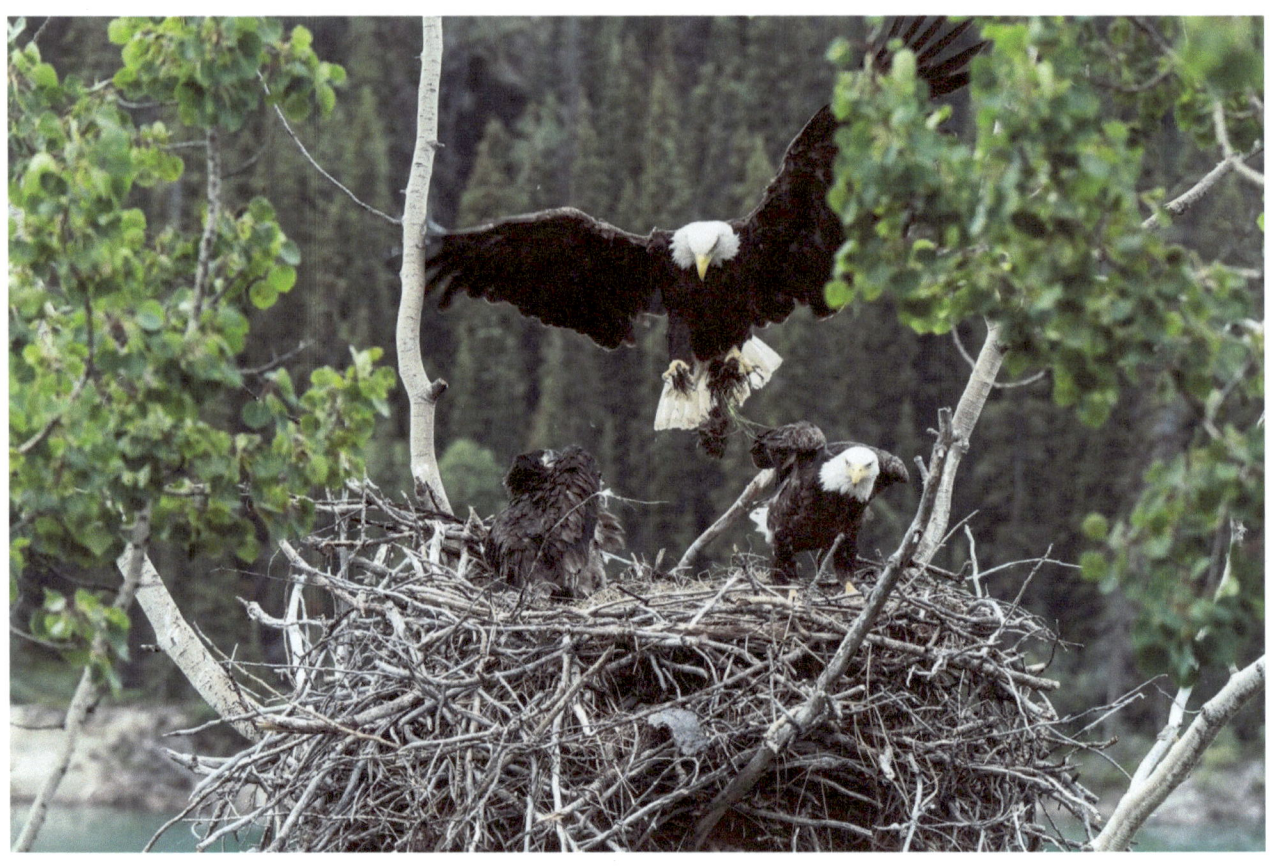

I was hoping for a fish, but instead dad has returned
with a clump of moss to put inside the nest to make
it more comfortable for all of us.

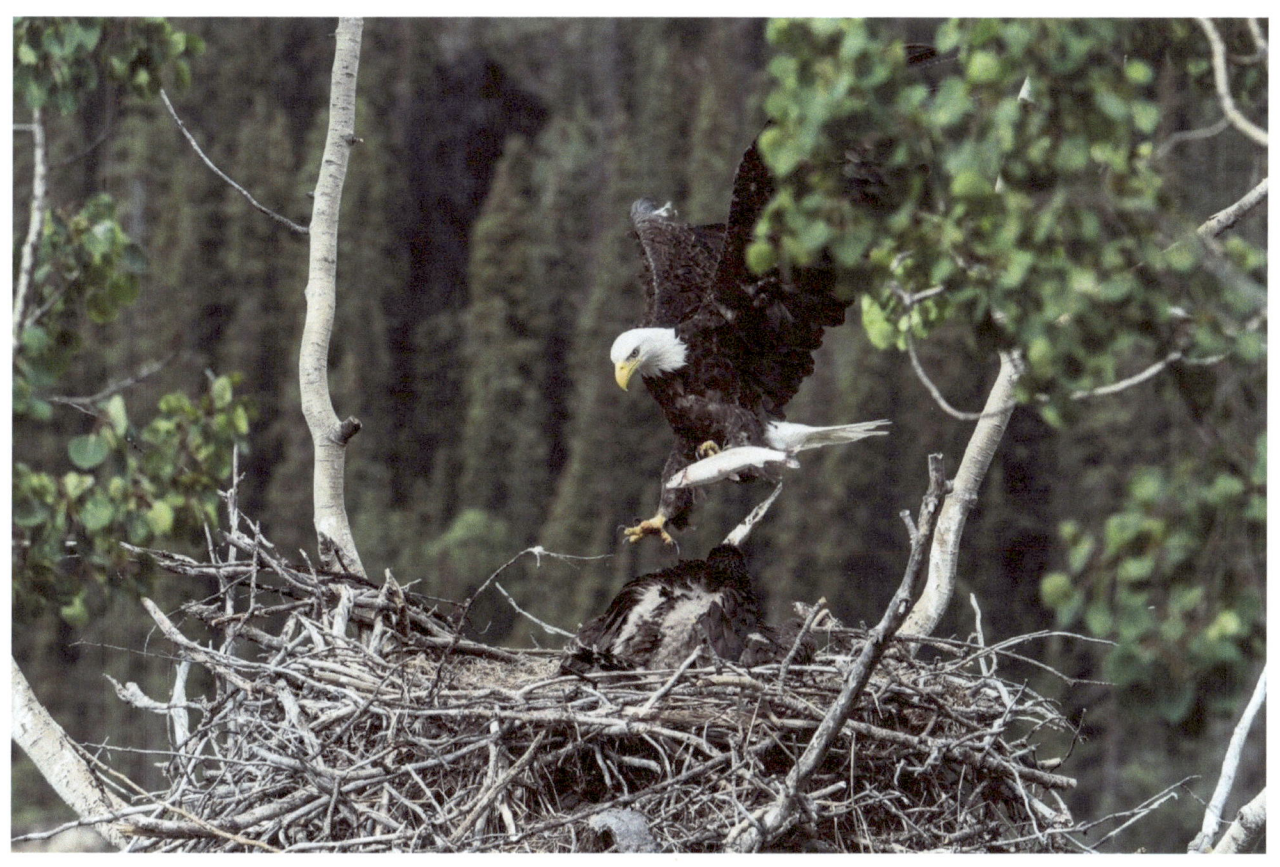

But a few hours later mom finally catches a fish and brings it to me. It's about time!

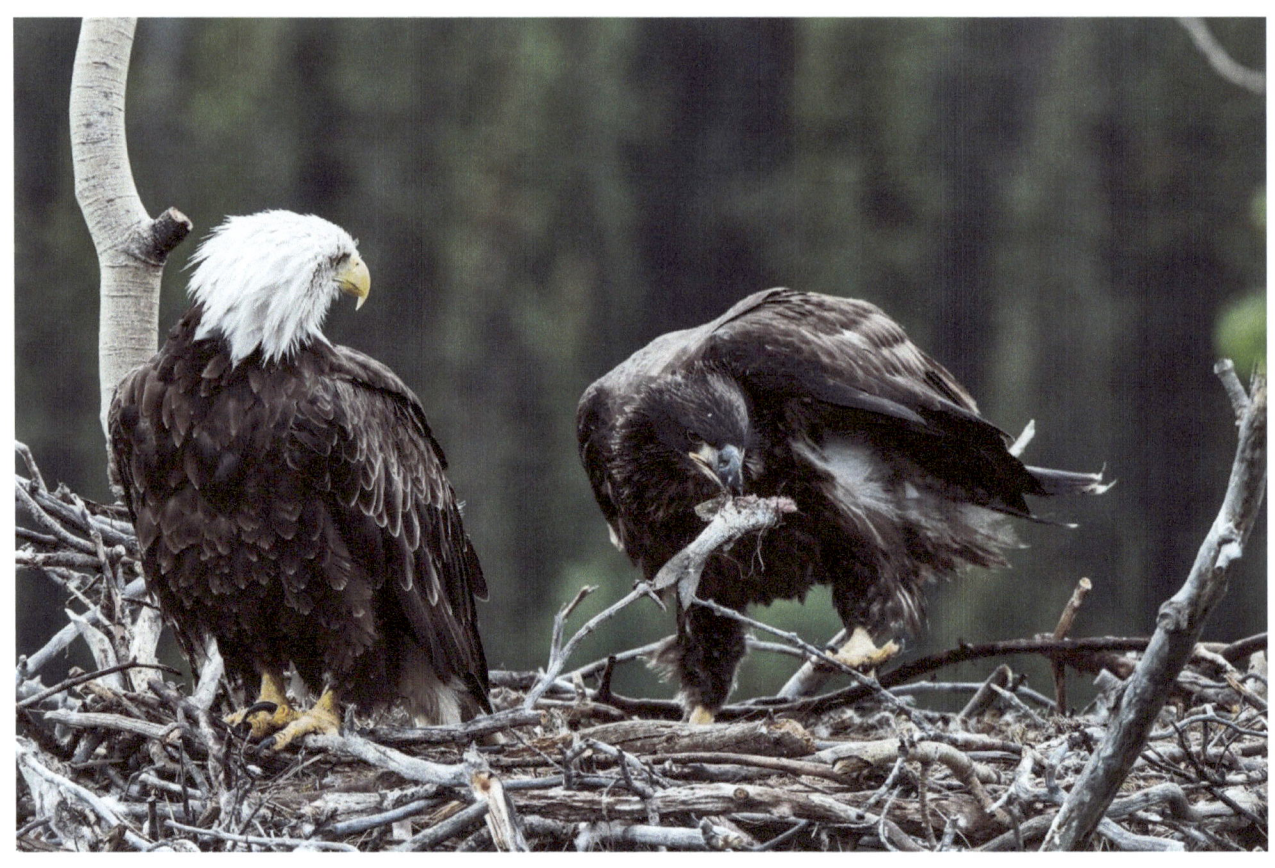

Since I am older now, I try to eat the fish without any help. I manage to bite off a piece but I'm not so good at feeding myself yet.

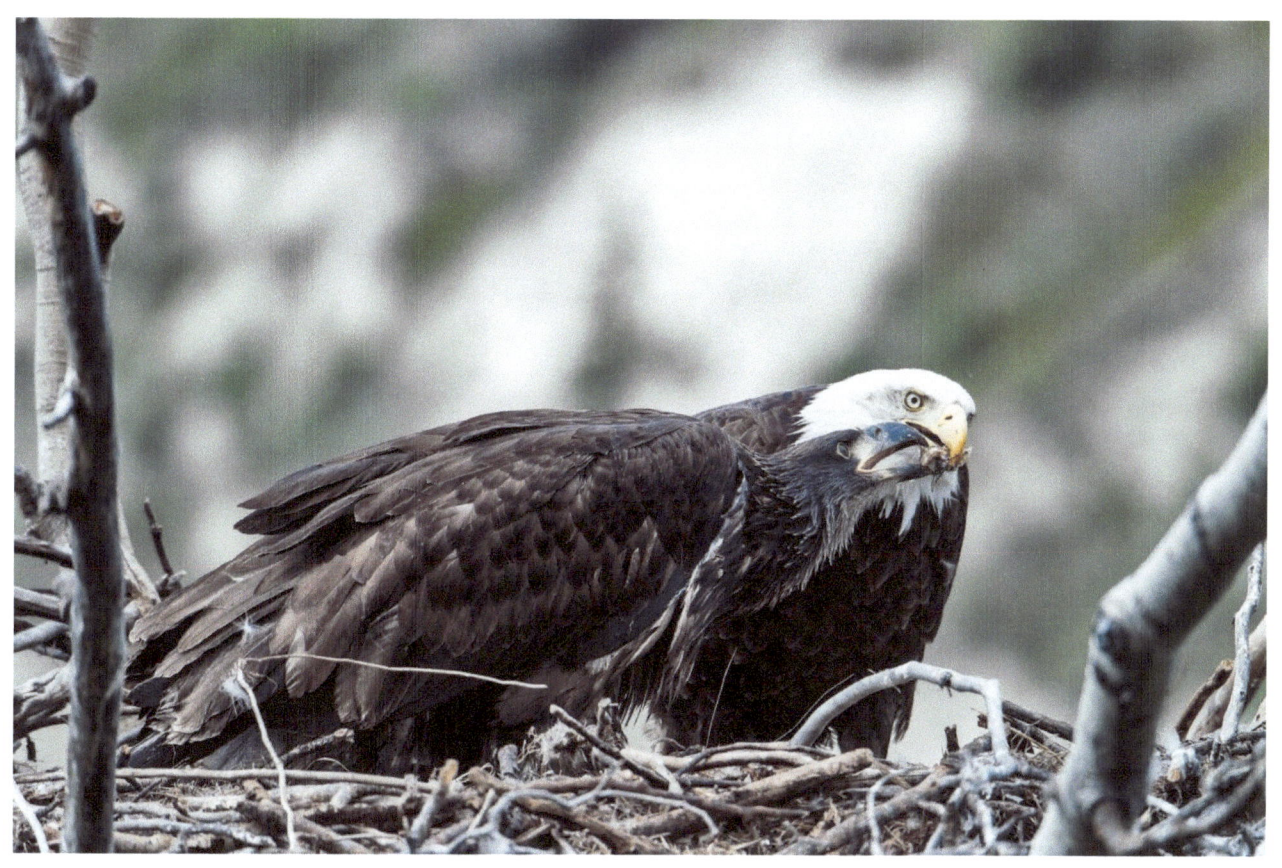

So mom bites off little pieces of the fish and carefully feeds them to me. Someday soon I will learn to eat on my own.

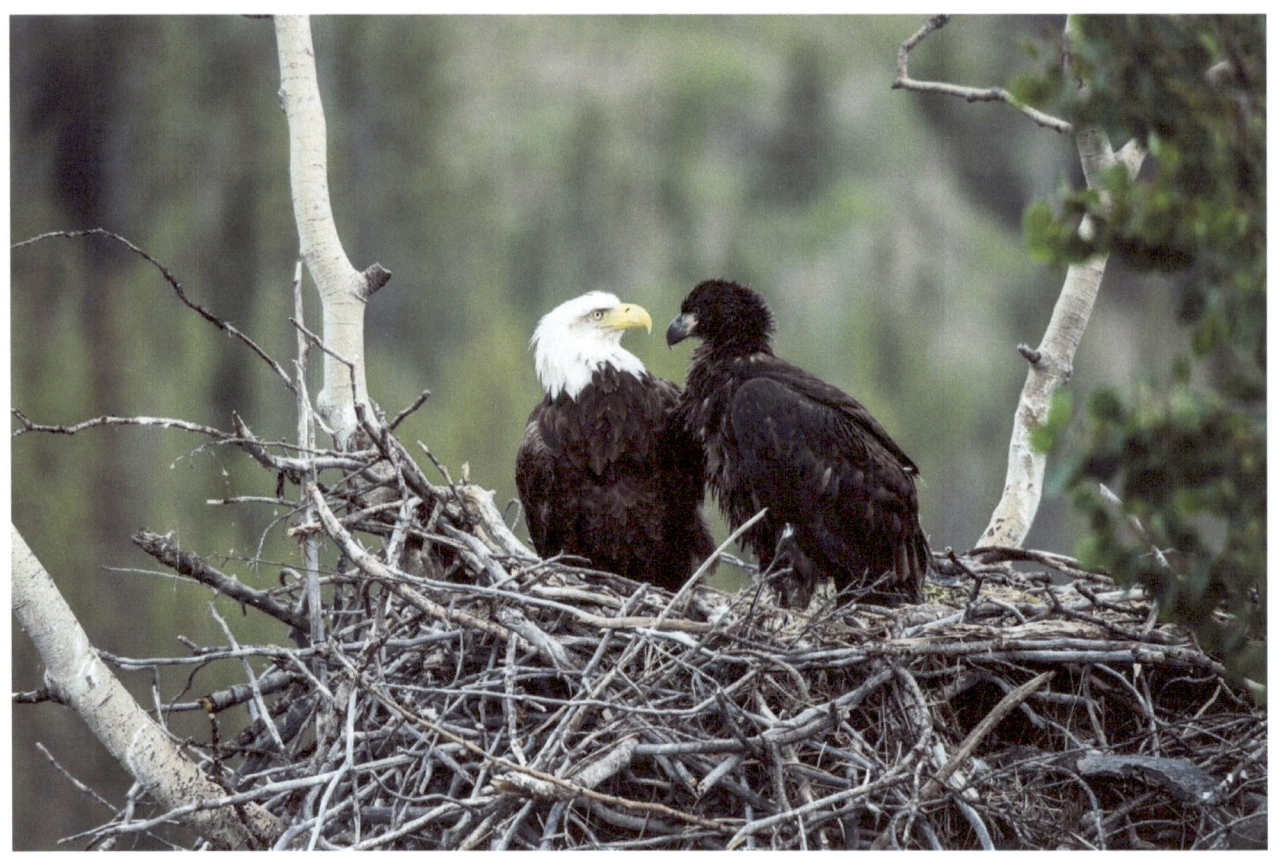

I am over two months old now and just about the same size as mom. She weighs about thirteen pounds and I am almost as heavy as she is.

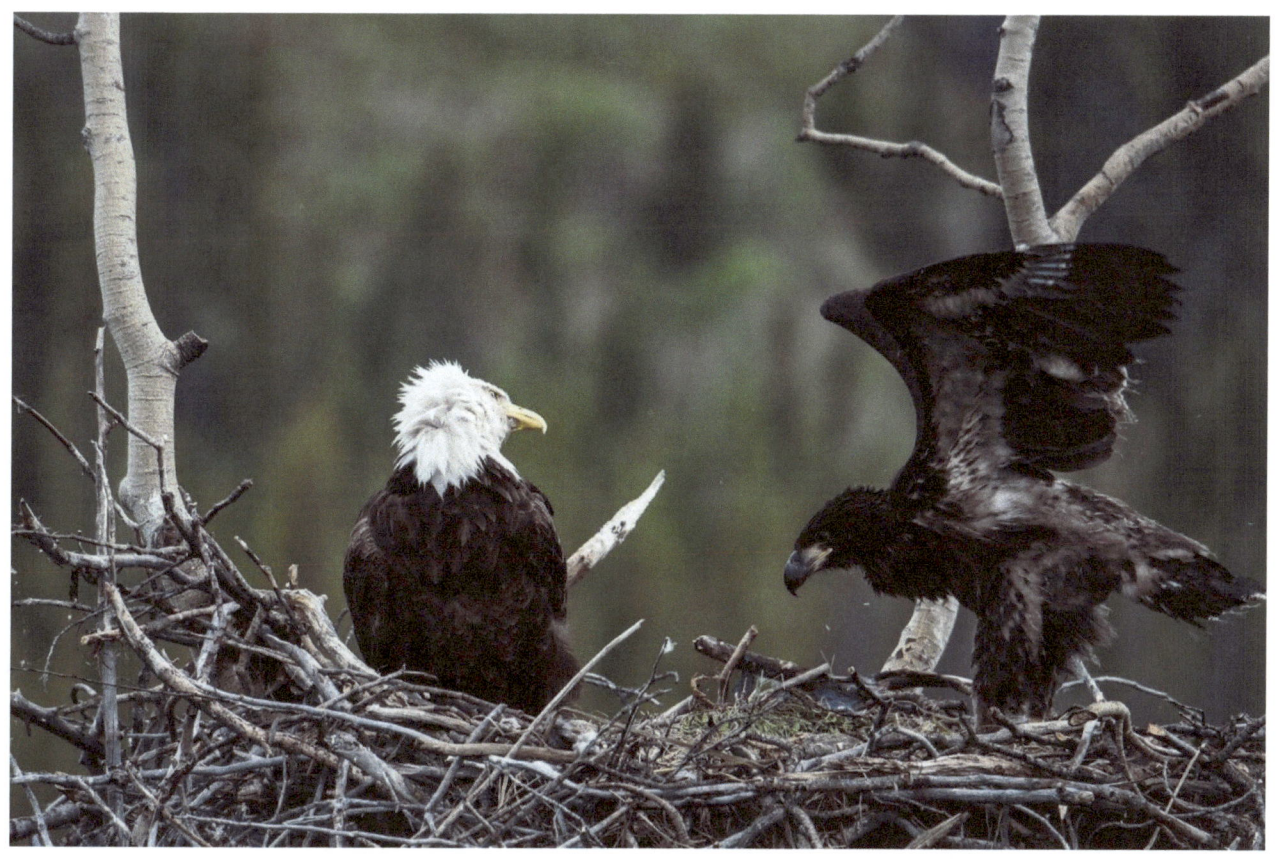

All my big feathers have filled in and I like to flap my wings to give my muscles some exercise. I am getting to feel grown up. But I still can't lift up into the air when I flap.

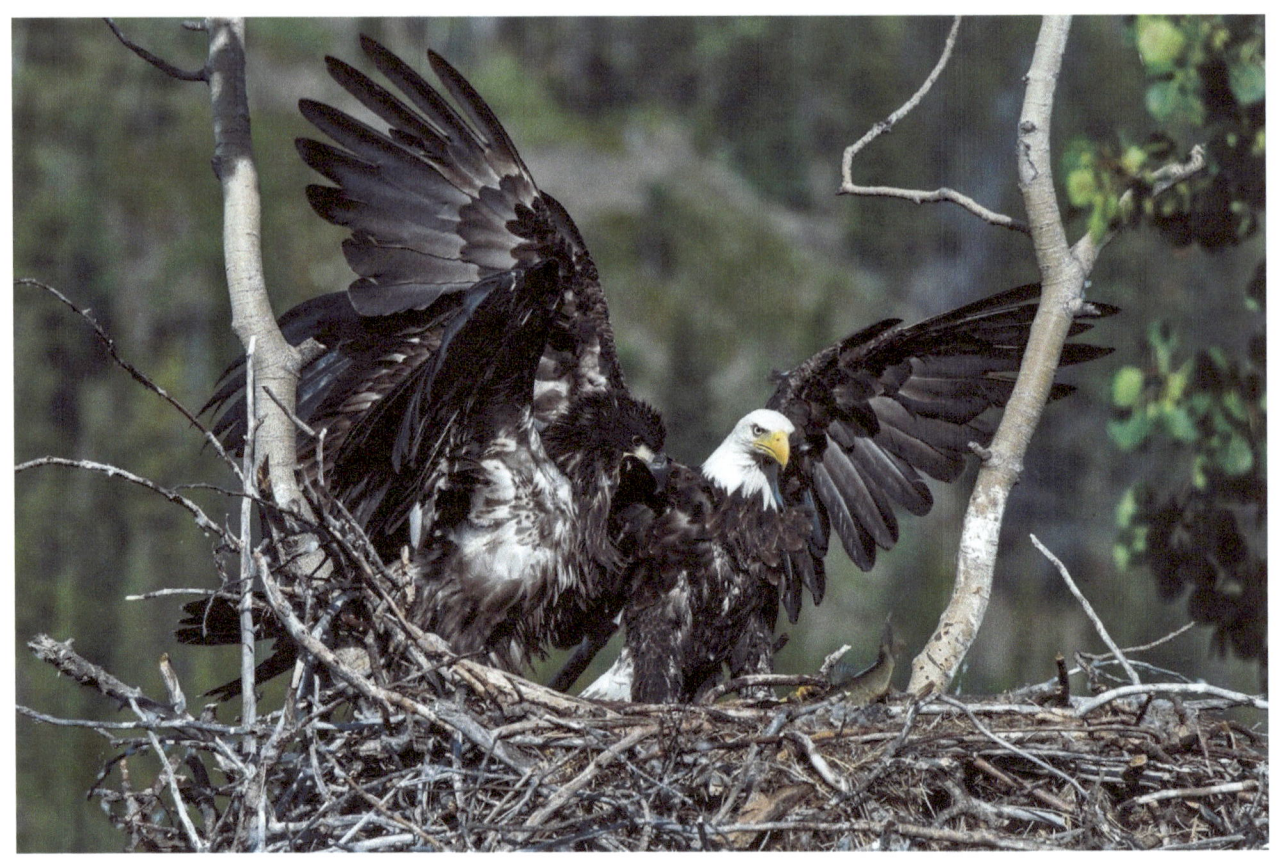

My dad's wingspan is about seven feet. When we spread our wings there is barely enough room in the nest for both of us!

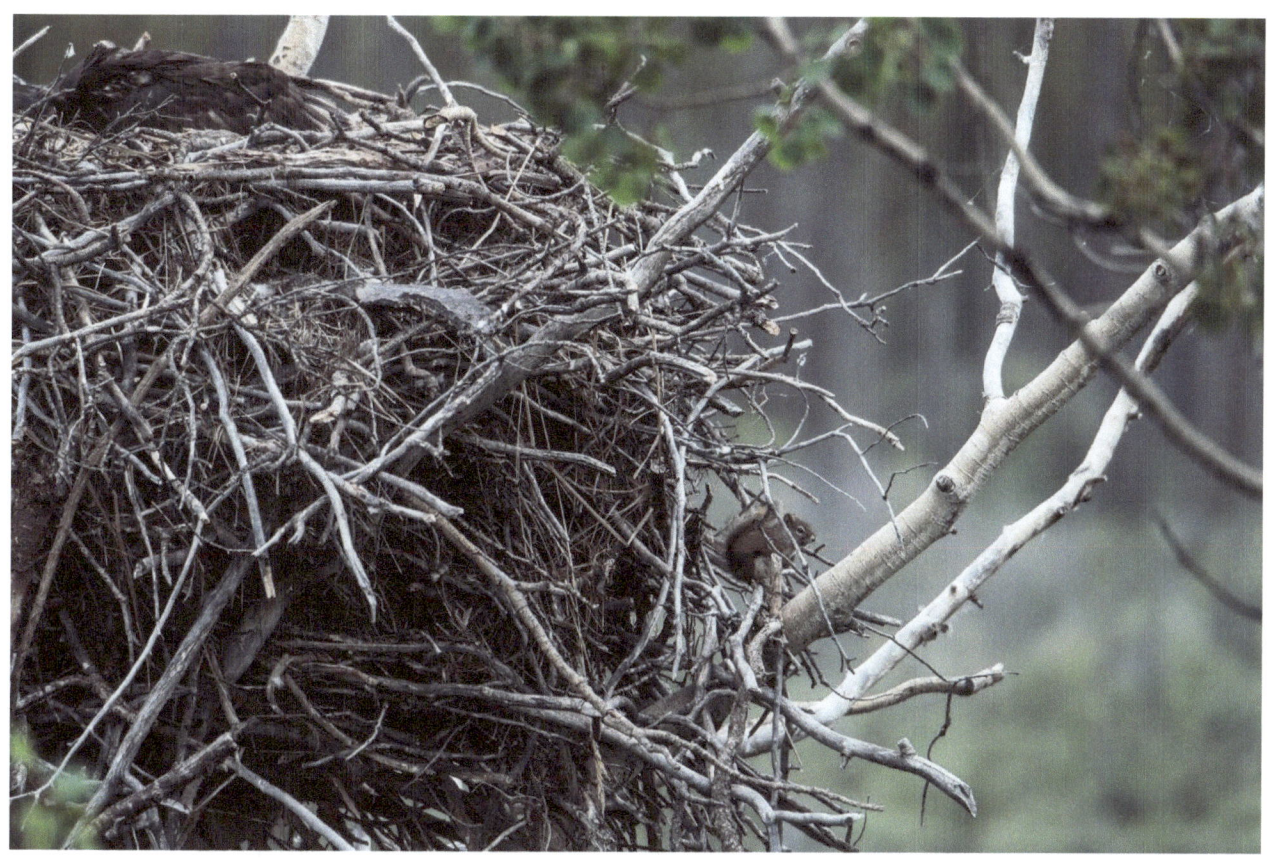

A little red squirrel likes to visit the bottom part of the nest. He climbs through the sticks and branches and sometimes chirps. I don't know if he is hiding any pine cones inside the nest for his winter food supply.

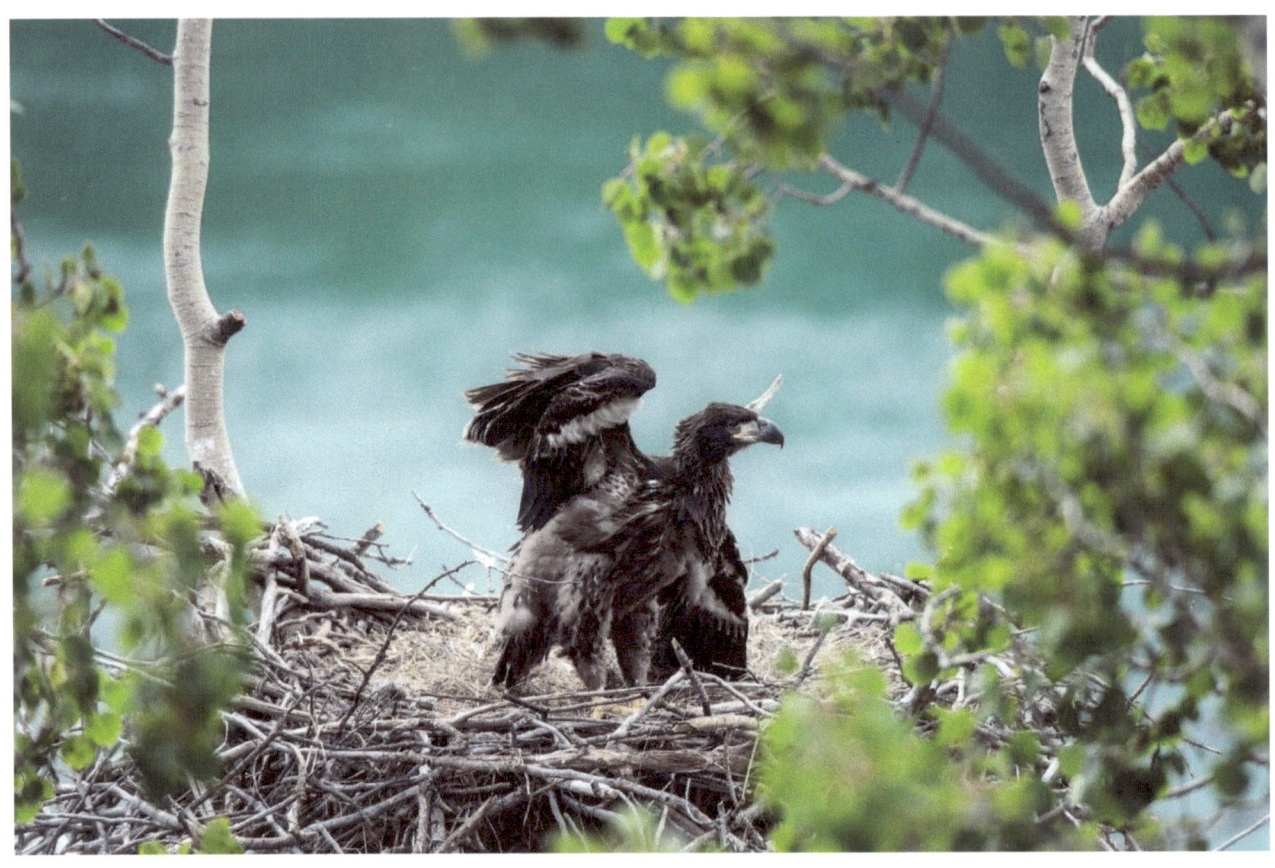

When both my parents left me alone today I started practicing to use my wings some more, but I got off balance and almost fell over.

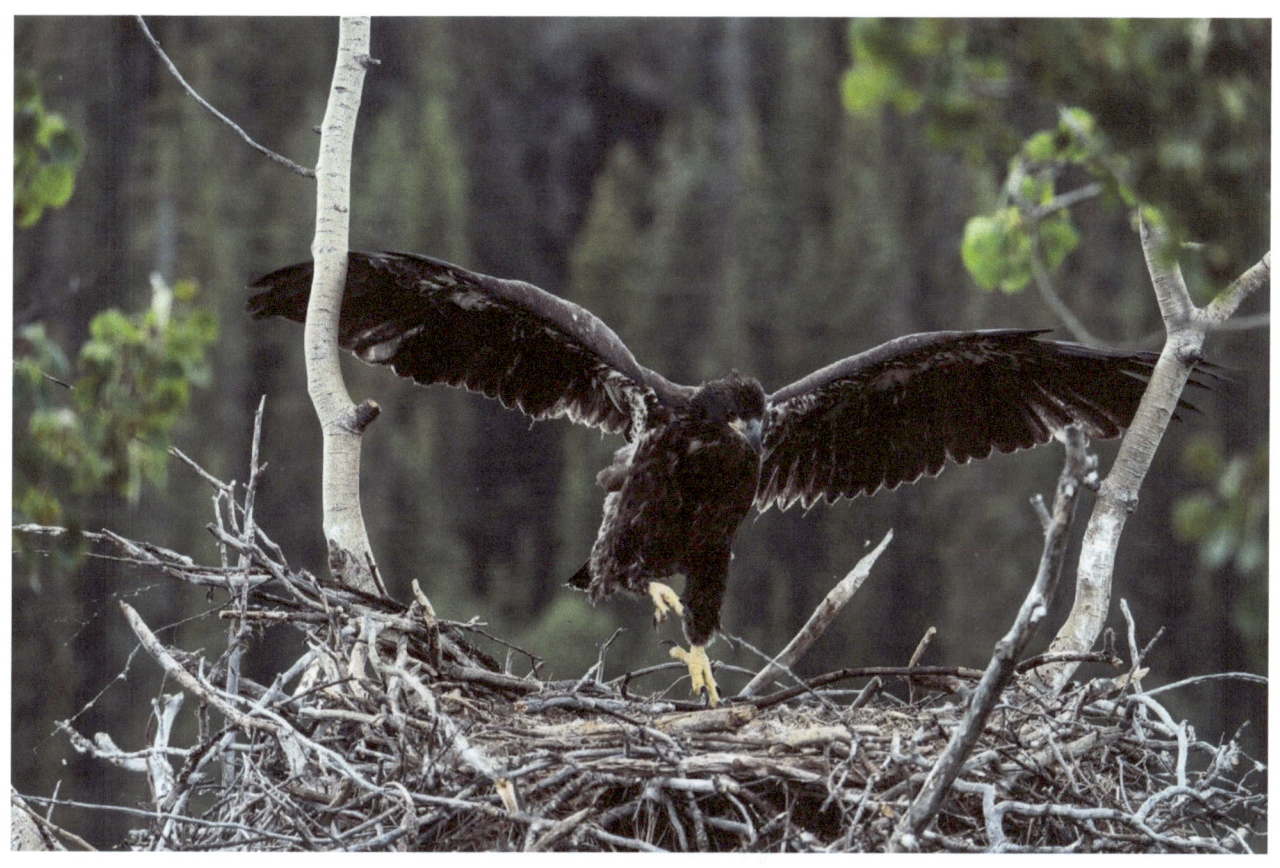

I kept trying and trying to get into the air and after flapping really hard I lifted off a few inches. It's not easy to learn how to fly. But my parents will expect me to start flying in another week or two. I hope I can do it!

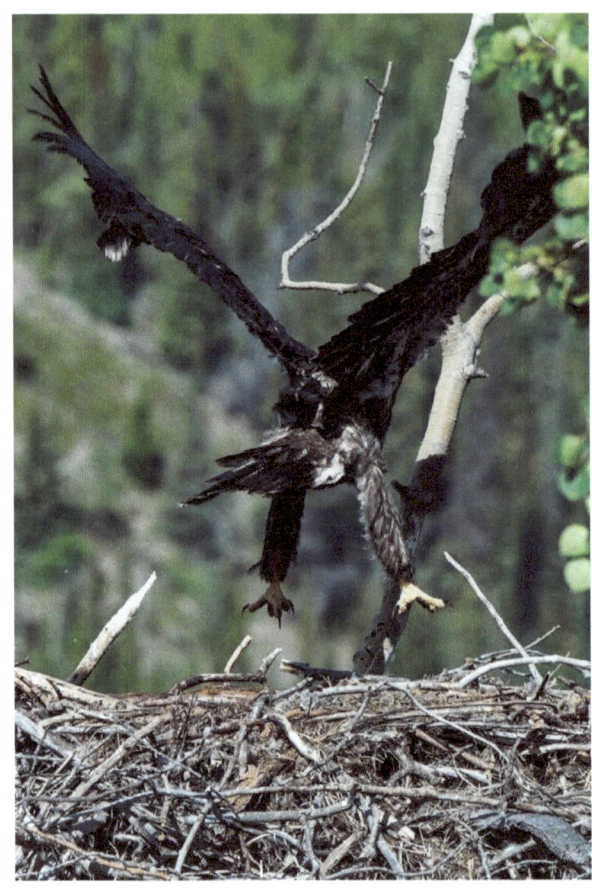

The following week I went a little higher. Each time I practice I go straight up like a helicopter and then come straight back down into the nest. I'm careful to not fall over the side.

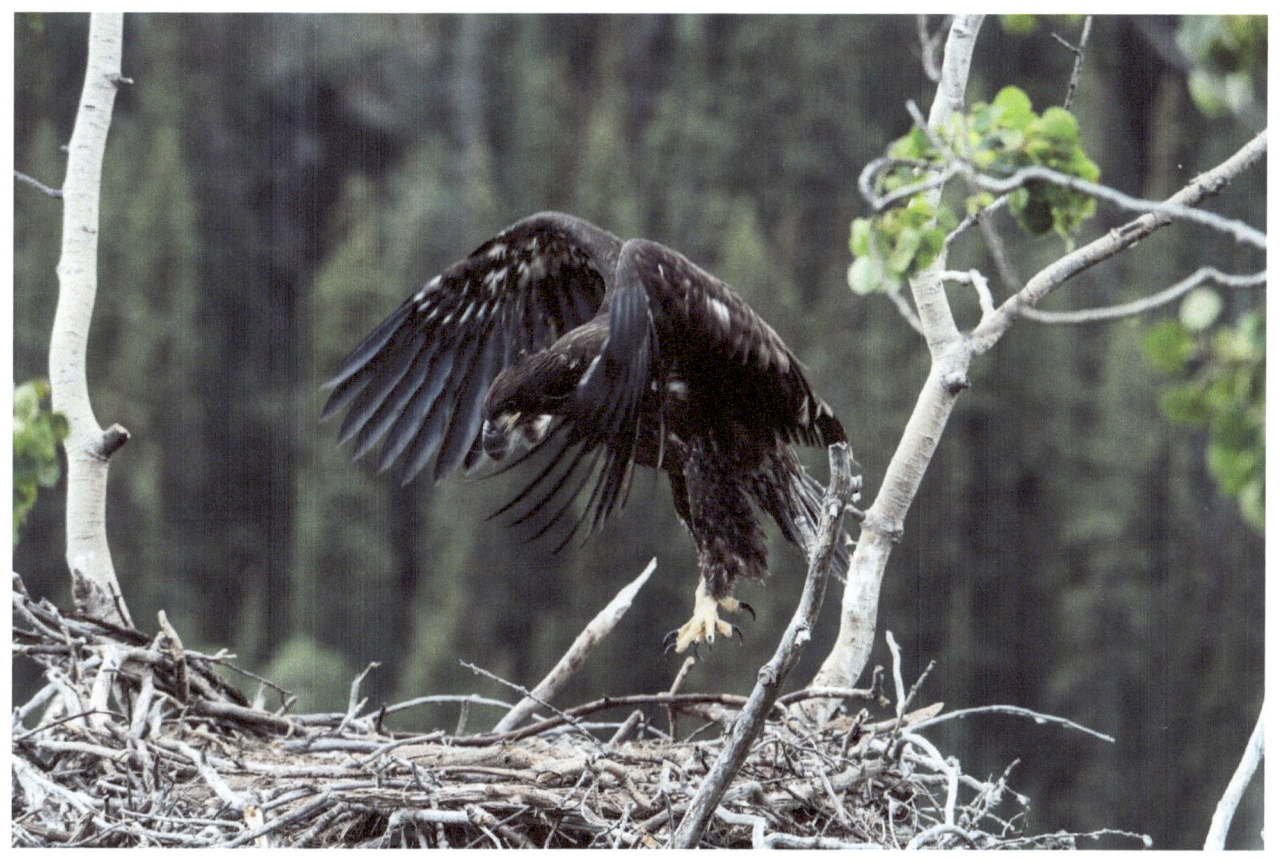

With lots of practice I am getting better. I lifted off more than a foot in height today. Tomorrow I will try to be brave and to fly out of the nest for the first time.

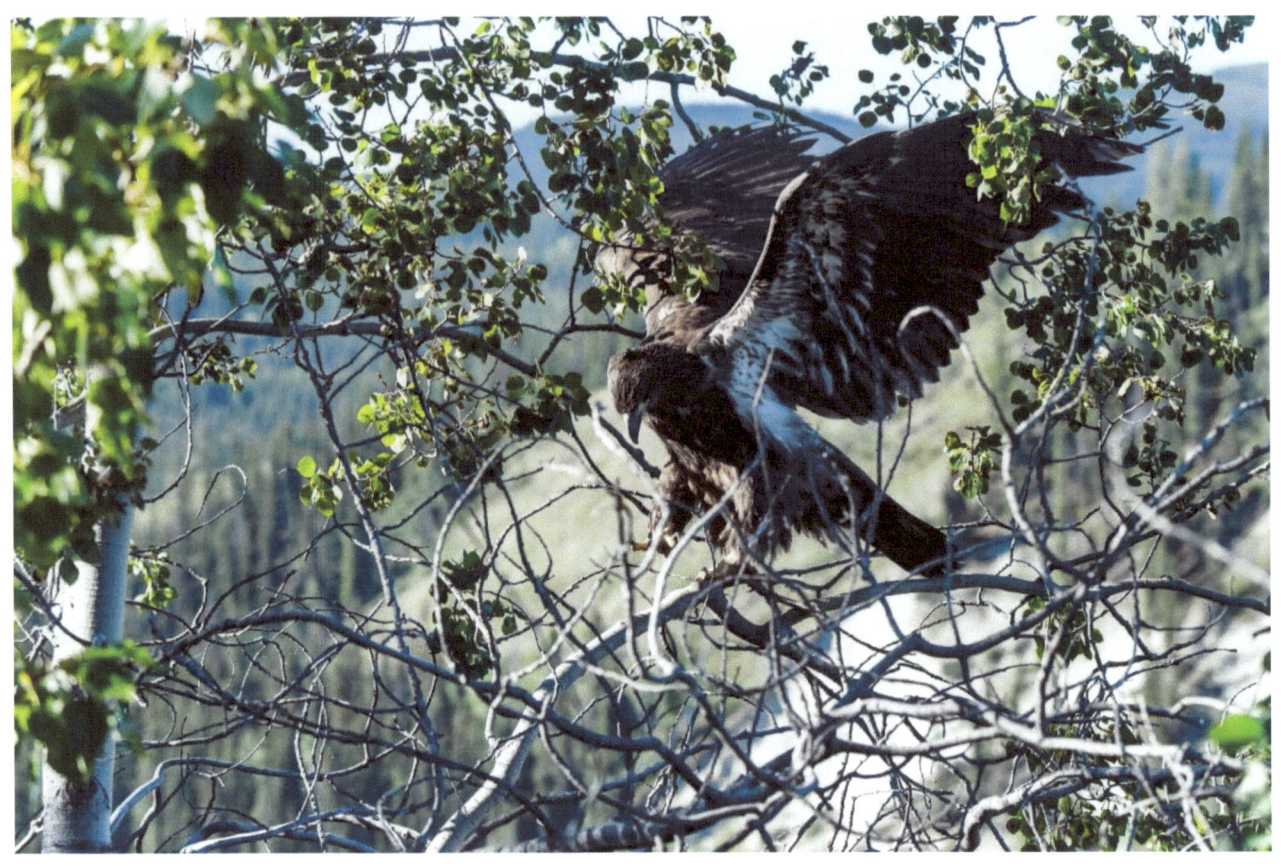

I did it! I flapped really hard and swooped into the branches of a nearby tree. I got a little tangled up but I didn't hurt myself.

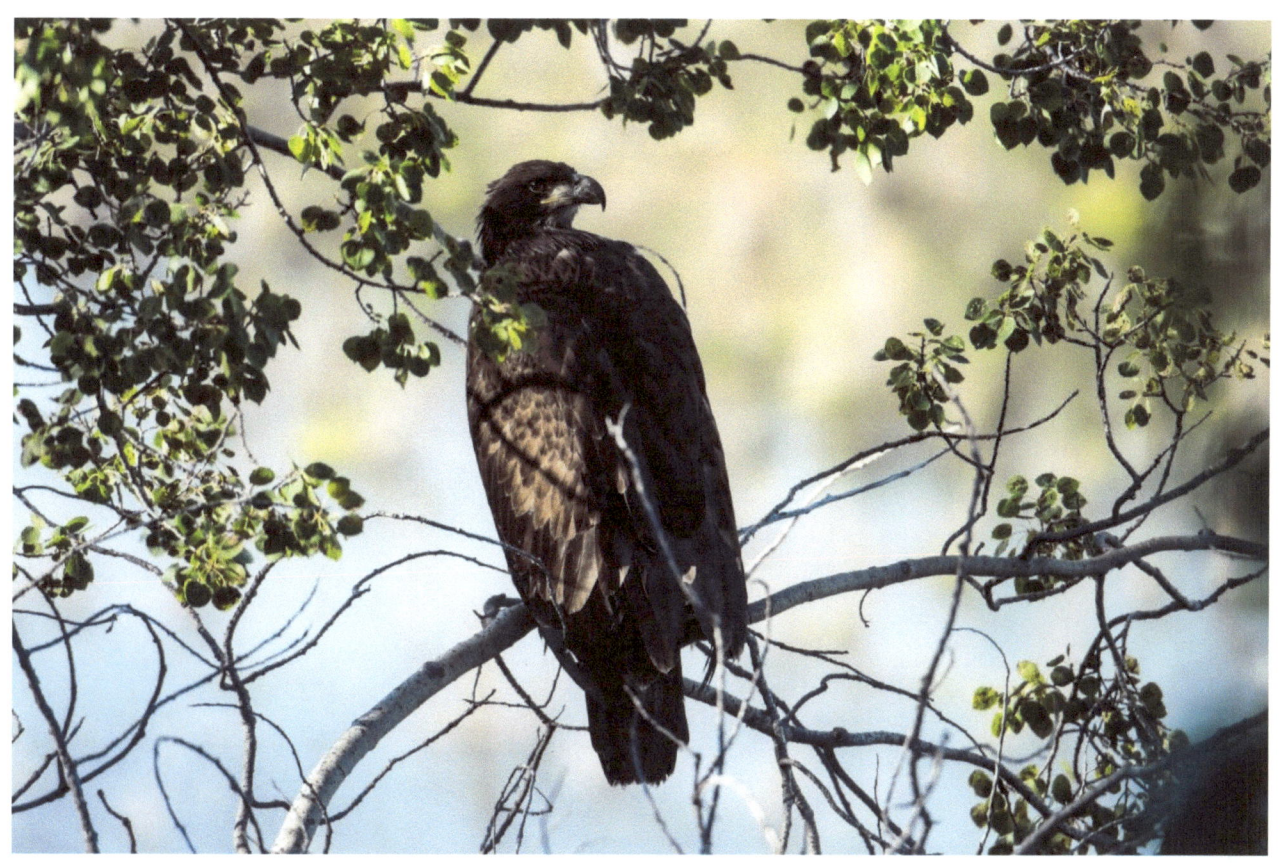

I pulled myself together and rested on a branch for about two hours. I could see my parents resting on a cliff off in the distance about a half mile away.

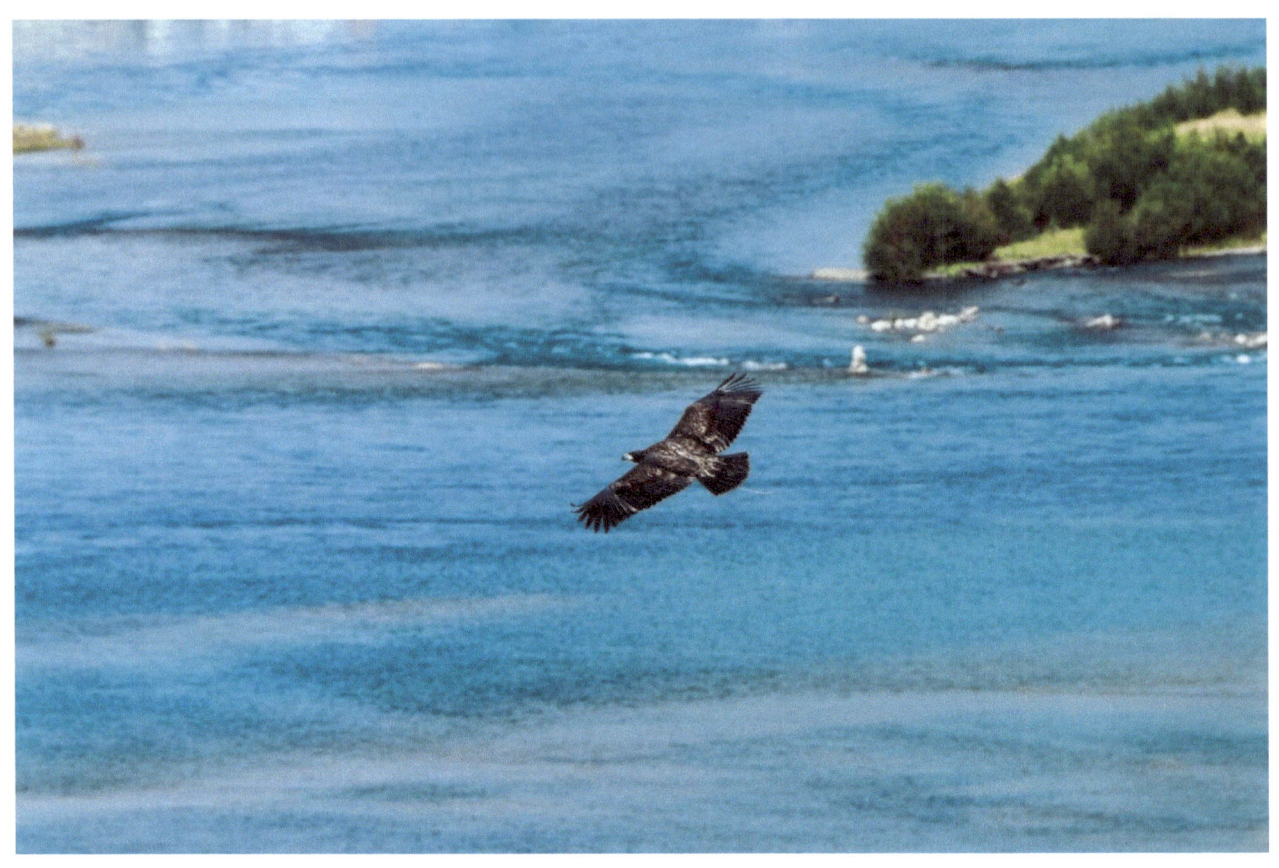

Finally I felt brave enough to let go of the tree branch and swoop far over the river below me. My parents were sitting and watching from their distant perch.

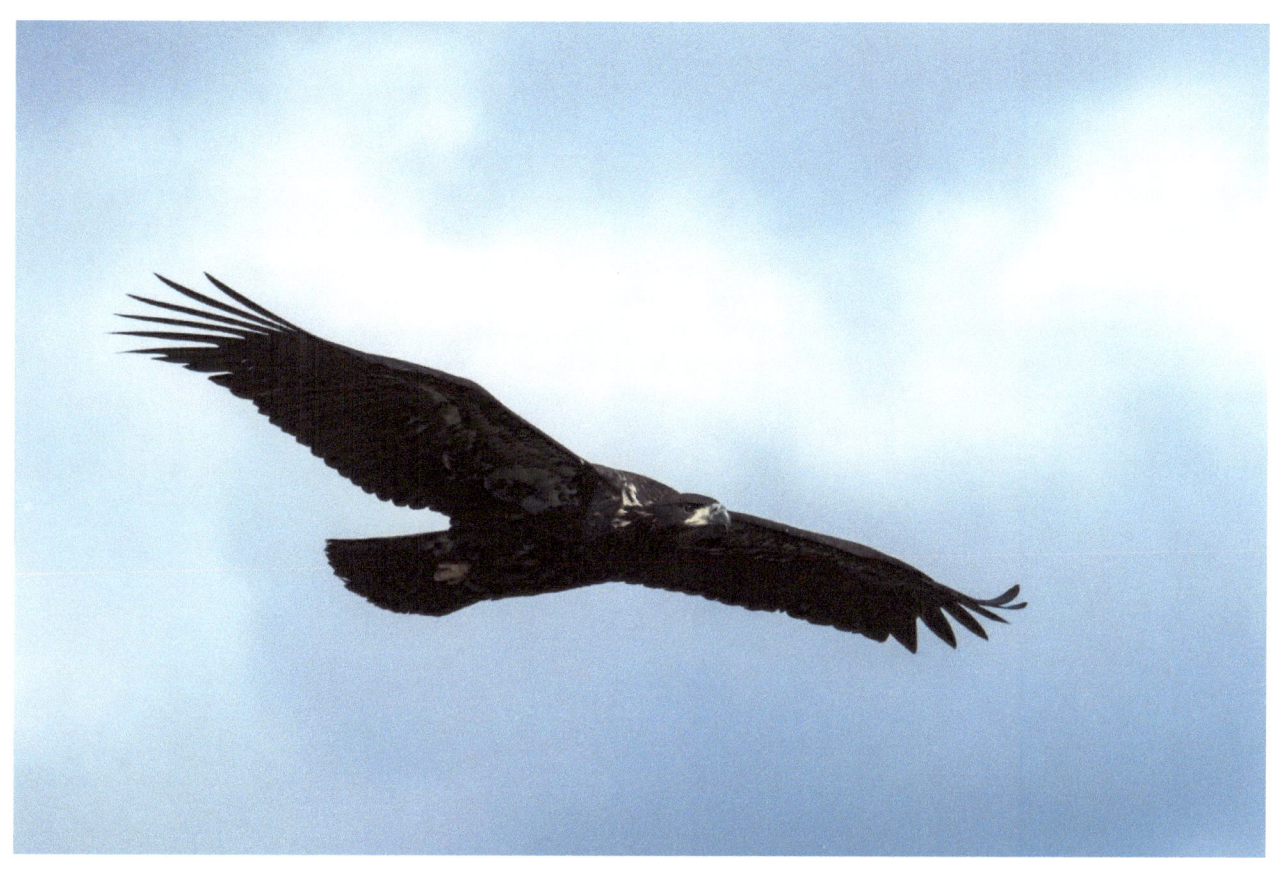

They must have been very proud to see me flying. They had raised me so that I could go out on my own, and after sitting in that nest for thirteen weeks I was so excited to be soaring way up in the sky.

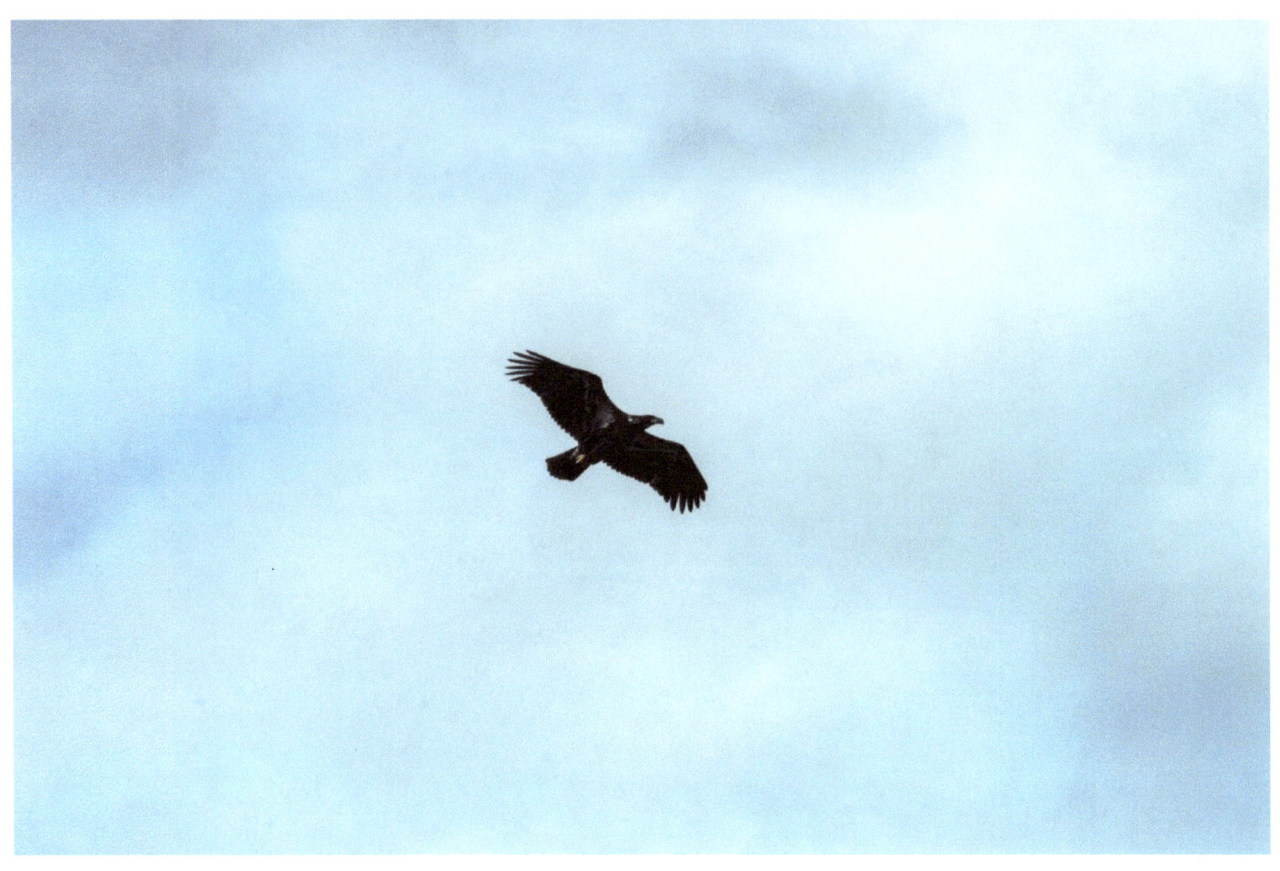

I still have a lot of growing and learning to do and I won't have a full white head and tail until I am five years old. But now I can follow my parents and they can teach me how to fish and how to be an adult eagle. What a great summer this has been!

Author's Note

I've been observing bald eagles in various locations ever since moving to Alaska in 1981. But it was not until the spring of 2014 that I had the opportunity to photograph eagles while they were nesting. Friends made me aware of an active nest just below a high cliff that overlooks the Yukon River in western Canada. The vantage point was perfect for photography, looking right down into the nest from fifty feet away. And fortunately the eagle family totally ignored my frequent presence, so I did not need to be concerned that I was disturbing the birds.

I returned to the nest site weekly throughout the spring and summer, until the second week of August when the young eagle flapped its wings, lifted off, and began a new phase of its life.

It was a privilege to be able to observe, close up, the development of the eaglet and its interactions with its parents, starting just after hatching in the beginning of May, until it fledged thirteen weeks later and joined its parents soaring overhead in the vast Yukon sky.

The images in the book portray this first summer of the eagle's life.

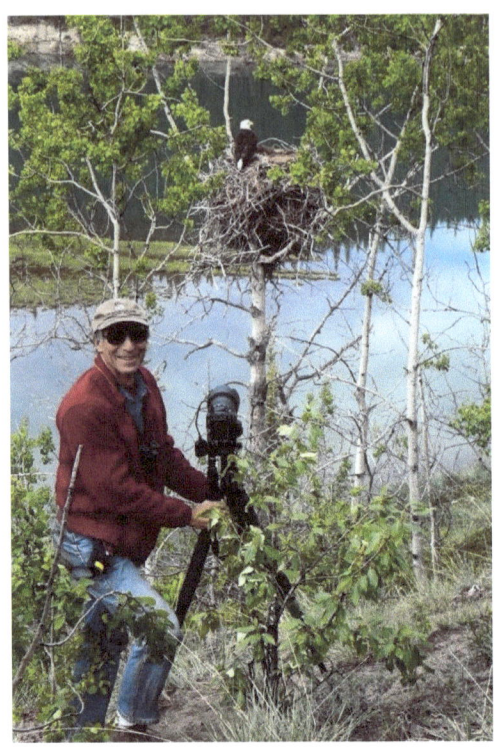

photo by Dennis Senger

Mark Newman's photographic work has appeared in worldwide publications for forty years. This is his twelfth book. His children's book, *Polar Bears*, won the Bankstreet College of Education 2012 Best Book of the Year Award as well as receiving commendations from the National Science Teachers Association, National Council of Teachers of English, and the School Library Journal.

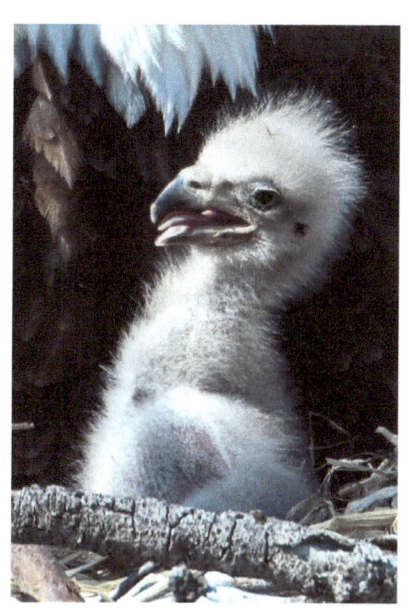